About the Author

Anthony Amaral brings to his latest book, **Mustang: Life and Legends of Nevada's Wild Horses,** a wealth of personal experience and research. As a recognized authority on the subject of horses and horsemen, he has achieved a wide reputation with his books and magazine articles.

Amaral is the author of four published books: **Comanche: The Horse that Survived the Custer Battle** (Westernlore Press, 1961); **Movie Horses: Their Training and Treatment** (Bobbs-Merrill, 1967); **Will James: The Gilt Edged Cowboy** (Westernlore Press, 1967); and this current book. A fifth book on horsemanship will be published in 1977 by Winchester Press. Amaral's biography of Will James was selected by the New York Public Library as one of the 100 best books for young adults in 1967. In addition, he has written some 300 articles for national and regional magazines.

Born in Yonkers, New York, Amaral "went west" in his late teens, working as a buckaroo and horse trainer and taking time out to earn a B.S. degree from California State Polytechnic College of Pomona.

The Lancehead Series

Nevada and the West

Books in the Lancehead Series

Retreat to Nevada: A Socialist Colony of World War I
Wilbur S. Shepperson, 1966

Diamondfield Jack: A Study in Frontier Justice
David H. Grover, 1968

Silver and Politics in Nevada: 1892-1902
Mary Ellen Glass, 1969

Restless Strangers: Nevada's Immigrants and Their Interpreters
Wilbur S. Shepperson, 1970

Mustang: Life and Legends of Nevada's Wild Horses
Anthony Amaral, 1976

Mustang

Other Books by Anthony Amaral

Comanche: The Horse That Survived the Custer Battle
Westernlore Press, 1961

Movie Horses
Bobbs-Merrill, 1967

Will James: The Gilt Edged Cowboy
Westernlore Press, 1967

Mustang

Life and Legends of Nevada's Wild Horses

Anthony Amaral

with illustrations by
Craig Sheppard

University of Nevada Press
Reno, Nevada—1977

Library of Congress Cataloging in Publication Data

Amaral, Anthony A 1930-
Mustang: life and legends of Nevada's wild horses.

(The Lancehead series: Nevada and the West)
Includes bibliographical references.
1. Mustang. 2. Wild horses—Nevada. 3. Wild horses—Legends and stories. I. Title.
SF293.M9A45 599'.725 76-53821
ISBN 0-87417-046-X

University of Nevada Press, Reno, Nevada 89557

Printed in the United States of America
Designed by Dave Comstock

For these Nevadans —
Wallace I. "Bob" Robertson and Robbie,
Albert Laird and Nell,
and Lillia Pepper

Contents

Author's Note

Probably nothing in Nevada better reflects the free outdoor life than its wild horses and the men who chased them. Both horses and men were *cimarrones*—the wild variety of tamer counterparts. The contrast made them the stuff of legends, to be gilded in that manner which gave the West in the age of horses its particular flavor.

When Mark Twain as an example tells of his Nevada adventures in *Roughing It,* and says "One of the most pleasant and invigorating exercises one can contrive is to jump across the Humboldt River till he is overheated, and then drink it dry," he is magnifying his reaction to a river that was a mere trickle compared to the Mississippi of his previous experience.

Similarly, when Nevada mustangers came together around a campfire in that less hurried age of horse culture, and one told of a stallion that had escaped his lariat, the disclosure if made without explanation would degrade the storyteller's talent as a roper. But if he said the stallion was the fleetest he'd ever chased (or the most beautiful, the wisest, or the most strong-winded) it would pardon the raconteur's failure with a rope and create a tale about a horse.

Like Mark Twain, mustangers would embellish a story, for that was the best way to tell it. And if the stories told about wild horses are not always historically accurate, they are historically correct in that they reflect the people who told them. Anyone who denies this aspect of the folk memory, and pursues only facts with rigid documentation, is chasing western history on one leg. Mary Austin, in her perceptive writings on the desert, expresses this idea best: "No man," she says, "has ever really entered the heart of any country until he has adopted or made up myths about its familiar objects."

In Nevada, wild horses gave great moments to the tongues of the mustangers, inspiring a lustrous folklore tradition. No other animal lent itself so vividly to the imagination. Neither the buffalo nor the antelope, western grazers of a true native wildness, had the power to evoke such marvelous tales. But wild horses, free in body and spirit, were heightened in these essences in comparison to those tame and bound by leather to man. The untamed became the totem animal of the American West.

Even today *wild stallion* is a liberator of mind pictures of a proud and beautiful horse, statuelike on a hill or bluff and wild as his surroundings. He is a leader, while below graze his obedient mares. He can race the wind, is a ferocious fighter, and only ear-catching names such as Thunderhead or Wildfire befit his splendid image.

If these majestic images were seldom captured in the flesh it is because they existed most fully in myths. But I am not an iconoclast in this particular instance. I enjoy an adventuresome horse story as much as those old men who delighted in telling them to me. And if I sensed in them a romanticizing of their youth and past vigor as horsemen, I listened, nonetheless, with enchantment; feeling in their tones a melancholy which said that their way of life was gone forever. Their stories and their experiences, genuine or spurious, were the color and emotion of their lives. To remove the passion would do them no justice.

However, the complete disregard for historical facts found in some western writing must be eschewed. The wild horses, for instance, that live in the hills less than fifteen miles from Nevada's state capital, and east and north and south in Nevada's mountains and deserts, are no more representative of the Spanish horses introduced into America in the fifteenth century than current cowboys are representative, in soul and substance, of the old-time range riders. Yet there are cowboys who believe they are, as others believe that these wild horses are pure Spanish mustangs.

Wild horses have changed in blood and type. In some instances degeneration has created ugliness. I have seen horses with heads more fitting for a 2,000-pound draft horse than their own 600-hundred-pound bodies. Others could stand as models for virtually every conformation fault known in horses.

Still there are some beauties. They can touch you with an emotion that is easier to feel, and more satisfying to see, than describe. Rudyard Kipling's Kim condensed it into the adage: "The wise man knows that horses are good." I am not sure if he meant the same thing I feel. I also like the saying: "There is something about the outside of a horse that is good for the inside of a man." This was proven to me when I first saw wild horses running free on a still summer day.

I was with a group of Pyramid Lake Indians out in the hills above the lake. The day was deathly quiet, and hot waves shimmered above the heat-dried desert brush. Five Paiute Indians rode to the higher peaks and disappeared into steep canyons to locate some of the herds that roam the reservation hills.

About an hour later a low rumbling crept over the stillness. Suddenly the volume became louder and there they were: about ten horses following a white leader, running recklessly down the long, broken slopes toward the blue of Pyramid. The landscape was vibrantly alive.

To see them, running wild and untouched by man, gave the country around me a special beauty and sent my pulse racing. In that moment I was a thousand miles from civilization.

Later, from another herd, the Indians skillfully roped a seal-brown stallion. He wouldn't rate for ribbons at a horse show, but his particular beauty was in the way he fought: rearing, grunting against the ropes, wanting to be free. For me there was more beauty in his struggle, and the reason for his struggle, than in all the trained antics of tame horses. I also knew then how easy it would be to make up stories about wild horses.

Nonetheless, stories of wild horses today do not carry the flavor of those told fifty odd years ago. This book is, then, an account of the horseback mustangers and follows wild horse history in Nevada to the advent of the Taylor Grazing Act of 1934. With this new order on the range came the last great wild-horse roundups in the West. Those drives witnessed the transition from the more emotionally charged chasing of mustangs from the back of a saddlehorse, to the detached and dispirited pursuit from airplane and flatbed truck. In that moment, when men stepped out of the saddle and into the cockpit, they stepped out of the age of horse culture.

Carson City, Nevada
1976

Anthony Amaral

About the Artist

Noted artist Craig Sheppard provided the illustrations for *Mustang*. The black and white sketches were done specifically for this book, and the color reproduction is from an original watercolor by the artist.

Craig Sheppard first earned his reputation as one of the foremost painters of the Southwest. In 1947 he founded the Department of Art at the University of Nevada in Reno. His western works and the paintings drawn from stays in Europe are represented in the Paris Museum of Modern Art, the Brooklyn Museum, the Gilcrease Museum, and other permanent collections. He makes his home in Reno.

Acknowledgments

For bibliographic assistance I am grateful to Michael Harrison for suggestions given, and to Nancy Bowers of the Nevada State Library and Pamela Crowell of the Nevada State Museum who helped uncover many items for me. Nell and Albert Laird and Lillia Pepper saved me countless hours by browsing through thousands of Nevada newspapers for articles pertinent to wild horses.

Thanks go also to Lura Tularski, Jewell Martin, Frank Robbins, Harry E. Webb, Wendell and Peg Wheat, Archie Dewar, Al Erwin, Jean Taylor, and many others for varied contributions that helped make this book.

A special appreciation to Bob Robertson and W. W. Hutchinson on whose knowledgeable shirttails I have unabashedly ridden.

A.A.

1

East and West of the Great Basin

The only true wild horses that inhabited the Western Hemisphere mysteriously disappeared about ten thousand years ago. But North America, their evolutionary cradle, saw a sixty-million-year development from small, dog-sized, three-toed animal to the horse of the present. Hernán Cortés, wading his precious sixteen horses onto the shores of Mexico in 1519, was never to know that he had returned the horse to its ancient nursery.

Spanish horses were the most esteemed in sixteenth-century Europe. They were a blending of indigenous Spanish types with horses of Moorish Africa. To understand Nevada's wild horses, historically and those of today, one must know something of the Spanish horse and its diffusion into North Africa.

After the Moors were driven out of Spain in the fifteenth century, a significant element of the Moorish heritage retained by Christian Spain was the sleek, desert-bred horse called the Barb. He is only slightly heard of today and is often confused with that other, more refined, desert horse, the Arab.

Far more romanticized than the Barb, the Arab is frequently hailed as the ancestor of today's wild horses. This is a bit of nonsense still favored in popular stories. That the Arab horse was the main blood influence in the creation of the Spanish horse is comparable to the fable that Arabian warriors overran Spain in A.D. 711 (it was really North African Zenetes).

Doubtless some Arab horses were taken to the Iberian Peninsula for the use of chiefs, or imported after the conquest of Spain. Mostly, however, it was the Barb. Variously described in chronicles as African, Moorish, and Barbary, his fiery, excitable nature—his "hot blood"—was crossed with "cold-blooded," draft types in Spain. And just as Arabs crossed with cold-bloods in England a couple of centuries later produced that marvelous hybrid, the Thoroughbred, so the cross between Iberian and North African desert horses gave rise to the Spanish horse.

Yet we know little about these horses except for the praise they aroused in equestrian centers throughout Europe. Decades later when Spanish horses were running wild on the American plains and were called "mustangs," their special virtues intrigued Americans on the Atlantic seaboard. Patrick Henry sent for the best and most pure Spanish breeds west of the Mississippi in the Pawnee country. Thomas Jefferson, a man of insatiable interests, wrote to one of the first mustangers, a man named Philip Nolan, for information on these horses running wild in Spanish Texas.

Judging by the equestrian portraits of the Spanish nobility, the Spanish horse was a type that today's western horsemen might call a "good little horse"—typically reticent, but expressive of high esteem.

ii

The Spanish horses that went wild in the southwestern United States descended not from expedition strays of Coronado or DeSoto or Cortés—another popular fancy—but from Spanish settlements and missions. These colonies dotted the northern frontier of New Spain from Texas to California, beginning in 1598 when Juan Oñate and his contingent of soldiers, families, Indian slaves, missionaries, and livestock settled among the sedentary tribes in New Mexico. What happened in New Mexico was repeated throughout the settlements on the raw margin of the Spanish frontier.

The core of Spanish existence in the New World was ranching. Livestock grazed and multiplied on the open, unfenced expanses of the country. By 1630 New Mexico had twenty-five missions and sixty thousand converts in ninety pueblos. Feeding the Indians required enormous numbers of cattle and sheep, far too many to be herded and cared for by the Spaniards. Besides, many *caballeros* were not inclined to that menial task. About 1621 permission was reluctantly granted from higher authority to allow Indians to mount horses and perform as herders.

This license was a radical departure from Spanish ordinances that had forbidden the use of horses and firearms by the Indians, ordinances that recognized the Indian to be less troublesome if kept dismounted. But the missions, reported Fray Juan de Prada, could not exist without cattle, and cattle needed tending. The Indian was put on a horse and taught to ride and to herd.

This fact is clouded by another myth which claims that the Indian ran down wild horses on foot and taught himself to ride by simply imitating Spanish horsemen he had watched. It is possible, and no doubt the feat was occasionally performed. However, the real cultural transition from pedestrian to mounted status began at the pueblos when some Indians were taught horse management. They formed a nucleus of equestrian knowledge and eventually transmitted it to other tribes.

The Pueblo Indians, for example, were never content under Spanish rule and mores. The vaquero (herder), who worked most closely with the Spanish, was probably the first to become disgruntled. By the simple expedient of being mounted he had a newfound pride beyond the reach of a mere field hand. Pride progressed to rebellion. When he stole away to join the wild tribes beyond Spanish dominion, he *rode* away, and probably took a few extra horses with him!

"A man on foot is no man at all" was an Anglo saying, but it applied to any proud race of men who sensed the advantage of being mounted. The runaway who wandered into the domain of the wild tribes would be readily accepted because he had horses and knew how to ride. He could teach. With the teaching grew the profound awareness of the horse as wealth in hunting and warfare. And as each tribe saw another becoming mounted, its members were soon convinced that their own destiny demanded horses—however obtained.

The wild tribes rapidly learned that the church's padres, who no longer would dismiss the increasing number of runaways, were more than willing to trade horses for returned escapees. Acquiring horses in this manner, however, was too slow. A quicker method was to raid Spanish horse herds.

This was particularly so after the Pueblo revolt in 1680. The Spaniards were sent fleeing south toward El Paso, abandoning thousands of horses. The Pueblo Indians traded off the horses to adjacent tribes on the southern plains. These tribes in turn became the envy of tribes further north. In a short time mounted Indians, particularly the Comanche (who have been called Lords of the South Plains), were raiding into Mexico for horse booty. Even the Blackfeet in Montana, after they acquired horses, made forays into New Mexico for Spanish horses.

While captured horses were reshaping the cultures of Indians west of the Mississippi, escaped horses were multiplying at a phenomenal rate. On the limitless expanses that reached north into the Great Plains the mustangs were finding a perfect breeding ground.

iii

From the Spanish southwest frontier, the horse emigrated north through two main routes east and west of the Rocky Mountain hump. The eastern stream flowed north through Texas and New Mexico into the Great Plains, then widened eastward toward the Mississippi River. The horse migrated slowly on this eastern side of the Rockies, by spurts, as each of the many Plains tribes slowed the horses' advance until they had adopted the horse culture. By 1750 tribes on the Canadian line were mounted.

West of the Rocky Mountain divide—on the eastern fringes of the Great Basin (along the eastern Utah border)—the horse traveled northward more rapidly. Fewer intervening tribes and scant pasture speeded the herds along the Green River in Utah, then across the southwest tip of Wyoming and onto the rich pastures of the Snake River valley in southern Idaho. Horses arrived there about 1690 or 1700 and were an integrated part of Indian life on the Columbia Plateau by 1730.

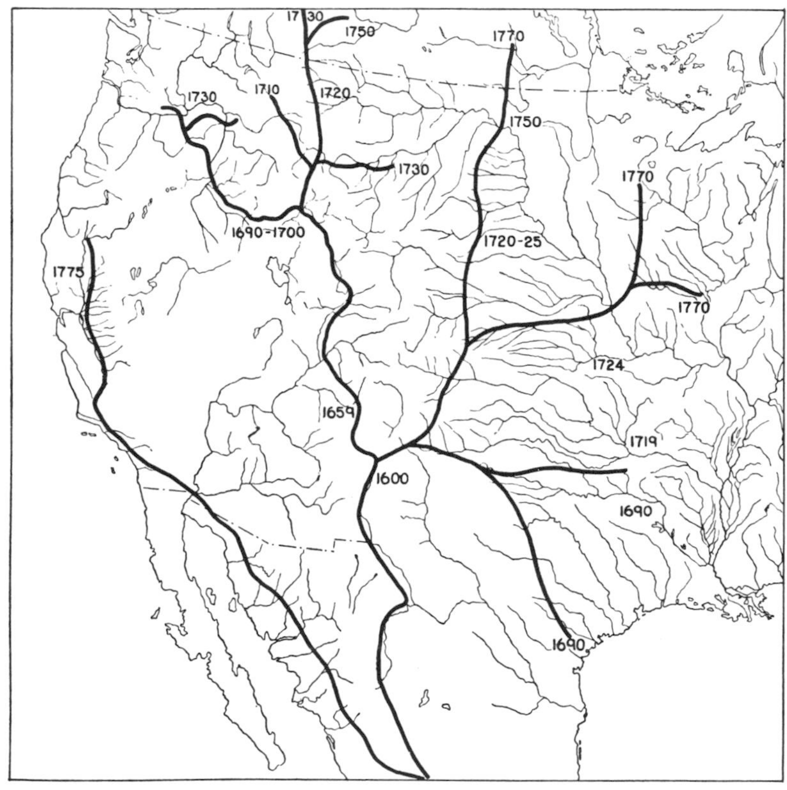

Map showing the northward spread of the horse in the western United States. Lines indicate the approximate routes followed by horses; the dates show the approximate time the horse reached each area. (From "The Northward Spread of Horses Among the Plains Indians," by Francis Haines, *American Anthropologist,* July-September, 1938.)

The far-ranging Shoshone were the traders who dispersed horses throughout the northwest regions. They bartered for horses, Spanish riding gear, blankets, and beads in Santa Fe. Through the Shoshone, neighboring tribes such as the Cayuse, Walla Walla, Yakima, Palouse, Flathead, and Nez Percé acquired their first horses. The Nez Percé, in turn, helped introduce the horse to the Blackfoot and Crow Indians on the northern plains.

By the time of first Anglo explorations into the plateau country north of the Great Basin about 1800, horses were plentiful within the tribes. Wild horses were still relatively few.

But west of the Great Basin, in Spanish California, wild horses were sufficiently numerous to be a competitive threat to cattle on the pastures of Spanish missions. California, like New Mexico, Arizona, and Texas, was settled by the Spanish through their mission system. From the outset California pastures provided mission livestock with abundant feed. The California prairie, central valley, and woodlands were rich in perennial bunch grasses—purple needlegrass, nodding needlegrass, blue wild rye, pine bluegrass, and deer grass. Most of all, the native grasses made California the "Pastures of Heaven" for supporting immense herds of livestock and wild game.

Mission statistics for about 1800 list 74,000 cattle, 88,000 sheep, and 24,000 horses. Perhaps even greater numbers existed. The land was unfenced and horses, particularly, roamed with minimal attention from the mission herders. An idyllic tempo and a casualness in livestock accounting were Spanish characteristics which carried over from the mission era to the rancho period.

These days of the ranchos were times when a man's land holdings were measured in square leagues and his horses might number four thousand head or forty thousand. It made little difference. There was hardly a market for horses. Thus horses in the San Joaquin Valley and on the Sacramento plains were allowed to grow wild.

Trapper-explorer Zenas Leonard wrote about the California prairies swarming with wild horses in the early 1830s. He described them as fat and of all colors.

Much later James H. Carson, a forty-niner who left his name at several diggings and wrote one of the more pleasing accounts of California during the gold rush, said that the Tulare Valley (now called the San Joaquin) "perhaps contains a larger portion of wild horses than any other part of the world of the same extent. On the western side of the San Joaquin [river] there are to be seen bands from two hundred to two thousand. These bands are to be met with at intervals from Mt. Diablo to Tulare Lake. The traveler, in going from the mouth of the lake slough to the head of the lake—four days travel—can see the plains covered with these fine animals as far as the eye can reach in every direction."

John Bidwell, one of the first Americans to settle in California, spoke in the same tone about wild horses in the San Joaquin Valley. Herds, he wrote, could be seen "twenty miles long."

Ranchers exterminated thousands of wild horses during drought to save pasture for cattle and sheep. During what Bancroft, the California historian, calls the "great drought of 22 months between rains" (1828-1830), about forty thousand horses and cattle perished. Some horses were purposely driven off the cliffs at Purisima. At Santa Barbara seven thousand horses were forced into ocean graves, repeating a similar slaughter of herds there in 1807.

When convenient cliffs were not at hand, men were employed to shoot wild horses. This was practiced at the San Diego Mission where wild horses passed by in droves, spoiling the pasture for tame horses and often taking the domestic stock with them. More barbarous was the custom of shutting horses up by the hundreds in corrals to starve.

Other settlements corralled all free-running horses. Branded animals were separated and claimed by their owners.

The *mesteños*—wild, unbranded—were prodded through a small gate of the corral, one at a time, and lanced by a mounted vaquero. Thousands were killed in this fashion.

The greater number of wild California horses roamed from the west side of the San Joaquin River into the coast range hills and valleys. Wild horses east of the river and toward the Sierra Nevada mountains—the western fringe of the Great Basin—had a later beginning when recalcitrant ranch owners evaded governmental edicts to slaughter their horses during drought. Instead, they drove their horses to the San Joaquin plains.

"But they [the ranchers] never went back and the horses bred like flies," wrote Johnnie Walker, a descendant of the Walker who served as guide to Captain John Frémont. "That is why so many wild horses sprang up all at once in California and that is why there were so many when the Americans came."

About twenty thousand wild horses roamed the San Joaquin Valley. These California horses, like the *Californio* way of life with its *no se apure* (don't be in a hurry) overtones, were alien to the Americans. Old-style Californios were overrun, scattered, or absorbed. California horses and cattle disappeared even more rapidly, for later American stockmen saw little quality in these comparatively smallish animals. They were supplanted by so-called Yankee breeds of livestock, particularly a type of horse called "American," to be described later.

The native Mexican horse, wrote Titus Fey Cronise in the 1860s, "while of great endurance, light weight, and excels in steady liveliness, was not suited to the demands of the American settlers. American and half-breeds [American horses crossed on Spanish] are fast supplanting the native stock."

And the California wild horses, even more worthless in the eyes of American agriculturists and town builders, were slaughtered wherever found competing with cattle for grass or land. They fell prey to the same single-mindedness which poisoned the grizzly and shot out the native elk. What horses were missed were reduced to inconsequential numbers during the droughts of

1864 and 1872. Small, scattered bands were still seen, however, past the turn of the century.

iv

Meanwhile, the greater epic of the wild horse was unfolding in Texas. It had begun long before Stephen Austin brought in his band of colonizers or a fence post was staked into Texas soil.

Early maps of Texas labeled huge areas of land simply as "vast herds of wild horses." The greatest of Texas's wild-horse ranges were between the Palo Duro and the Salt Fork of the Brazos River, and between the Nueces and the Rio Grande. J. Frank Dobie suggests that perhaps one million wild horses roamed Texas.

In 1807, at Nacogdoches, a Spanish ranching center east of San Antonio, a military commander reported that his garrison herds had stampeded into the "infinite herds of mustangs." To his dispair, his soldiers were left afoot. The few horses remaining within the post were being used to chase down runaways.

About thirty years later, the mustangs caused Ulysses S. Grant, at the time a lieutenant with General Taylor's army on the Nueces River, to marvel, "I have no idea that they could all have been corralled in the state of Rhode Island, or Delaware, at one time."

To Thomas A. Dwyer, who left his London law practice in 1847 to horse-ranch on the lower Nueces River, Texas mustang herds were a magnificent nuisance: "Time and time again I have had to send out my best men to scare away the immense masses of mustangs (charging around and threatening to rush over us), by yelling and firing at them. Then the mustangs would wheel and go thundering away as Byron grandly describes the hundred thousand wild Ukraine horses in Mazeppa."

v

During those prime native-grass days in the regions beyond the Mississippi, the terms "wild horse," "mustang," "Mexican horse," and "California horse" referred to horses that carried full measures of Spanish blood.

"Mustang" was the Anglicized corruption of the Castilian word *mesteño*. It referred to an animal that belonged to the *Mesta,* an organization of stockmen which, among other functions, made claim to all stray livestock. The Mesta regulated range use; they enforced laws on brands, thefts, and distribution of unbranded stock found at large; and they directed that a rodeo be held to gather the strays.

Another equally corrupted Spanish designation for horses is maroon, or marron, from *cimarrón*. It never found wide usage in the Southwest, but is still part of range vocabulary in Nevada and the Great Basin. *Cimarrón,* while now designating the bighorn mountain sheep, originally meant any wild animal which had a tame counterpart.*

Less complimentary sobriquets were "broomtail," "willowtail," and "fuzz-tail," heard wherever wild horses were part of the landscape. These names described a characteristic condition which occurred when horses were forced to eat certain toxic plants.

"Locoweeds" *(Astragalus* and *Oxtropis)* were a serious range problem. Some varieties of locoweed are acutely poisonous and kill rapidly. Other types are less toxic, but accumulate in the body slowly, poisoning an animal into paralysis and eventual starvation. If an animal does survive, its brain cells may be impaired beyond recovery.

Hence, a "loco horse" was one that staggered about from brain damage. A locoweed-poisoned horse displayed his condition through an abnormal profusion of mane and tail growth, and this gave rise to such terms as broomtail. Today, the names carry facetious connotations of inferior horses, or are generic terms for wild horses.

---

* In strict Mexican-Spanish usage only such wild horses as the former "tarpans" of Europe and Przewalski's horse were *cimarrones*.

While the toughness of mustangs made them choice horses for some horsemen, they were a plague on the land to the settlers. Extermination of wild horses intensified as westward migration inexorably conquered the territory of the wild horse, the buffalo, and the Indian. And the constant removal of the better mustang specimens by shooting or capture left culls to breed to a deteriorated standard.

However, unlike the buffalo whose decimation was nearly permanent, the wild horse population continued to fluctuate. Settlers' horses (American horses—mixed types from eastern states) often got loose and joined with mustangs remaining in tucked-away canyons, isolated ranges, and mountain retreats. These horses too speeded the deterioration of the wild horse stock from the original Spanish mustang type.

Bob Lemmons, who chased wild horses in the Texas brush country during the last quarter of the nineteenth century, remarked: "A lot of times when you'd spot a bunch of horses, you'd think they were mustangs, but you'd find out you had horses that had just gone wild." Lemmons thus distinguished between Spanish horses and the sort known as American horses.

Frank Collins, too, distinguished between pure mustangs and other horses. He acquired his horse savvy on the Texas plains and noted that in the 1870s horses on the Panhandle's llano grew larger than the mustangs in south Texas. Some of the stallions in the former region weighed 1,000 to 1,100 pounds, 400 pounds heavier than the usual mustang. These heavier horses were credited by Collins to American horses lost or stolen by Indians from emigrant trains going to California. The stallions, he said, got loose and mingled with the mustangs.

And James Cook, who lived a varied existence for fifty years on the frontier, said that by 1800 almost all the Spanish mustangs had disappeared from the plains; just a few were to be found among the Indian herds.

Although the true mustang of pure Spanish origin was thus almost gone by the turn of the century, and entered the memorial league of the passenger pigeon just a few years later, the term "mustang" remained to mean any wild horse—including the horse of mixed origin that came to inhabit Nevada.[1]

2

The Horse Comes to Nevada

Possibly the first reported sighting of a wild horse in Nevada comes from John Bidwell in the narrative he wrote as a member of the first emigrant train to California in 1841. The wagon train followed the Humboldt for many miles until halting at the river's sink. There "we saw a solitary horse, an indication that trappers had some time been in the vicinity. We tried to catch him but failed; he had been there long enough to become very wild."[1]

Another early observation was made by Dan De Quille, a reporter on the *Territorial Enterprise* published in Virginia City, while on a prospecting trip in the summer of 1861. In the Stillwater Range, east of Fallon, his party saw seven wild horses feeding in a little valley. De Quille surmised that the horses were "American horses strayed from the droves brought across the plains by emigrants."[2]

If not a comprehensive indicator, the sources strongly suggest an explanation of the start of wild horse herds in Nevada and the type which would dominate.

A major reason lies in the ecology of the Great Basin area of which most of Nevada is the heart. This area was one of the last areas of the continental United States to be explored and settled. It did not attract Spanish settlement which would have brought in the Spanish horse.

Nor did the Spanish horse spread from Indian tribe to Indian tribe in Nevada as it had done on the Great Plains. The tribes which inhabited the inhospitable Great Basin, especially those deep in the interior (between the Humboldt and the Old Spanish Trail), were made up of the most destitute of all American Indians. They lacked large-scale social organization, being scattered over the desert in small, isolated bands. Encountering a horse, they would be more likely to devour it than to put it to any other use.

Their lack of familiarity with the horse was documented by some early observers. For example, Captain J. H. Simpson, who explored western Nevada in 1859, reported the attempt of a Paiute to mount a mule: "In mounting his mule, he invariably would protrude his legs through and between his arms while resting his hands on the saddle, and in one instance, in his attempt to mount this way, awkwardly tumbled off the other side."[3] Other Indians along the exploration route continued to amuse Simpson's party with comical attempts to become acquainted with the stock, indicating the apparent rarity of horses in the area.

Not surprisingly, white people of the time viewed mounted Indians as potentially dangerous, while Indians who had not taken to the horse were regarded as offering little threat. Thus many of the Basin Indians by this criterion were considered "docile."[4]

There were of course exceptions to this general rule in Nevada. Some Indians on the northern and western fringes of the Great Basin had obtained Spanish horses from the plateau tribes, whose territory was traversed by the northern migration routes of the horse into the Snake River country in the 1690s.

The horse adopted by these Indians was the compact, speedy Spanish horse. Over the years, the type deteriorated through rough usage and indiscriminate matings. The term "cayuse," which had originally referred to horses of the Cayuse Indians specifically, came to be a disparaging epithet for an undersized, scrawny Indian horse.[5]

Thus there were three types, considered distinct and recognizable at the time, which could be seen in wild horses: Spanish horses of good quality (from Mexico, California, and Texas), Indian ponies, and American horses.[6] The latter were most common in Nevada.

The "American horse" was a product of the multiple functions desired of a horse on an eastern or midwestern farm. Agriculture, the growth of cities, and commerce required strong horses to work in harness. On the farm, a horse to work in a plow, to be hitched to a spring wagon for a visit to town, or to jump onto and bring the cows in from pasture had to be of considerable size and malleable temperament. These demands brought into being the American horse. Quite easily, too.

About the time James Fenimore Cooper was struggling with his writing to offer a work strikingly American in spirit, eastern horse breeders more handily created the American horse by the simple expedient of labeling any horse with size, "American." The horses were a mixture of European breeds, predominantly cold-blooded draft types.

Breeding the American horse followed whim more than husbandry formulas. Poor roads and long distances often left no opportunity for farmers to be discriminate. They had to accept stallions that were locally available. Fifteen-hundred-pound stallions were commonly crossed with mares weighing seven to eight hundred pounds, the progeny perhaps mated with a pony, and that crossed back to a draft stallion.

The heavy importation of draft horses increased the average height and weight of horses until size became the principal trademark of the American horse. Regional pride also exerted itself. Eastern Canadian horses became known as Canadians; Vermont Drafts were horses bred in that northern pocket of America; in Pennsylvania, German farmers developed a seventeen-hand horse called the Conestoga. Thousands of these horses would haul wagons and people across the plains to California, Oregon, and Washington. Add to the above mixtures the English running horse. He stepped ashore and became the American Blood Horse.

From this inordinate mixture of types and bloodlines, some definite American breeds did develop, such as the beloved Morgan, compact yet strong, and the fast-trotting Hambletonian, pride of the country drag racer. But most of the emigrants' horses which escaped to grow wild and wooly in Nevada were of mixed breeding.

Spanish horses, mostly from California, added to the mixture as they were trailed through the Great Basin for markets further east. A fascinating narrative of one such drive is the account of a Dane named Jorgen Daniel Bruhn—adventurer, soldier, and artist—who arrived penniless in California in 1871. For a dollar a day he joined a band of forty-one Americans on a horse drive. Three thousand California horses which had been collected along the Kings River and on the San Joaquin plains were to be driven—of all places—to Texas. Texas was then as horse poor as they were with cattle following the Civil War.

Bruhn escaped from the American temperament which he found loathsome, and from the enormous cruelties he watched being inflicted on the horses, by writing letters to his family in Denmark (during his spare time after herding horses eighteen hours a day). On the crossing of the Sierra Nevada, Bruhn wrote: "The journey from the base of the mountains to the tops has taken us four days, and we have lost on the average twenty-five of the oldest horses every day. The poor animals, which have been accustomed to run about freely on the plains, were unable to endure the hardships of mountain climbing."

At least six hundred horses perished in the mountains. Some tumbled down the mountainsides into canyons, or had to be abandoned because of their utter fatigue. The party, with nearly twenty-five hundred horses remaining, emerged from the mountains near Bishop Creek in the northern Owens Valley of California. Two hundred more horses died in the desert east of the mountains. Eight hundred in all had been lost by the time Bruhn was reporting these counts in a letter from Unionville, Nevada. The trip had required five months. At Unionville Bruhn was dismissed along with most of the crew, since the horses were to be wintered on the desert.

What happened to the horses is not known. That some went wild and spent the rest of their lives in the hills is likely. Herding two thousand horses on a fenceless desert is virtually impossible.[7] If any of these California horses did go wild, they would not have been a startling sight on the landscape. By the 1870s wild horses were a visible and growing part of wildlife in Nevada.

Much of that contribution came from the forty-niners' swarming migration to the California gold fields. And a decade later the tide washed back into Nevada with the discovery of silver on the Comstock Lode. Thousands of people, and even more thousands of cattle and horses, funneled into the bonanza territory. By the time Nevada was admitted into the Union in 1864, ranching was firmly established in the northern and eastern parts of the state.

The demand for horses was almost limitless as mining camps and towns sprouted out of the beds of mineral wealth. The need for big horses to pull freight wagons and stagecoaches, or to haul the ore from the mines, set a pattern of horse breeding in Nevada. Soon, ranches were running thousands of horses on the open range, harvesting them when new mining rushes made their call for horses.

These ranchers, until World War II, prided themselves in developing a strain or prevalent type that often carried the name of the breeder and his reputation as a horseman. The Dixon strain of horses in Eureka County, or the Bob Steele strain in Clover Valley, south of Wells, were highly esteemed. These men, and dozens of others along the ranching belt of the Humboldt River, frequently dabbled in other enterprises, mostly mining. But it was for their horses that they wanted to be known. There was a special pride then which lasted as long as Nevada remained a horseman's world. Often these breeders spent fortunes developing a type of horse that combined their special preferences in ability, temperament, size, and even color. But performance and stamina were the primary criteria.

Tom Dixon, who came from Ireland to California and then to Nevada in 1869, ranched in Eureka County. He made claim to many springs in the great expanses of white sage flats in eastern Nevada. Later he extended his holdings to Long Valley, and to Fish Creek, Spring, Diamond, and Monitor valleys.

Dixon also had mining interests, but he lavished his attentions on his horses. Until his death in 1927 the Dixon horse strain was the widest known of Nevada strains. He shipped horses to California, Kentucky, and Texas. Army remount stations were consistent large-lot buyers of Dixon horses. He had nearly ten thousand head on his vast holdings and never less than thirty riders on his payroll.

Wild stallions, however, Dixon loathed, and his riders had standing orders to shoot any when seen. Dixon also warned he'd shoot any rider who happened to shoot one of his own stallions.

Dixon favored Shires and Percherons, which he turned loose to join with wild mares. He was also partial to Clydesdales, but considered them too big and too heavy for running out on the range. Hambletonians, Morgans, and some Irish stallions and mares were imported by Dixon for developing his strains of heavy and light work horses and saddle types.[8]

E. C. Hardy, another famous name in Nevada horse ranching, gained esteem on his Oasis Ranch in eastern Elko County. In the late 1880s he imported twenty-six Norman (Percheron) horses and Clydesdale mares and stallions, from an Illinois breeder, to develop his own strain.[9]

This emphasis on heavy draft-horse importations contrasted with the preference for light, wiry horses in the southwest. As late as 1920 the light saddle horse was not in favor as a ranch horse in Nevada, especially in the mountain ranching country of the Ruby, Lamoille, and Star valleys in northern Nevada. Ranchers favored the undersized draft horse for ranch work and developed this saddle type by crossing draft stallions with wild range mares. Draft blood contributed size and a quiet temperament, while the mares passed on their endurance and hardiness. The stocky offspring were excellent for roping heavy steers, rounding up cattle in mountain country, and performing chores through the heaviest snowfalls.[10]

"Very near and dear to the hearts," claimed one buckaroo of these chunky ranch horses.[11] Another rider, Jim McDermott of Elko County, said that the best horse he ever rode was Paddock, sired by a 2,200-pound Percheron out of a hot-blooded mare. Joe Johnson, best known in the state for his roping horses, recalled Rondo as his best horse. Rondo was foaled in 1899 out of the same breeding as McDermott's Paddock. Rondo weighed 1,100 pounds and stood sixteen hands. In Texas, these dimensions would have placed the horse between the shafts of a freight wagon. But tastes were individualistic. Charles Clubine, another old-time rider, obtained his best saddle horses by crossing mares of various bloodlines with a French Coach stallion.

Virtually all ranchers stood their pet stallions at stud to outside mares, so spreading the influence of the particular stallions. Often, too, the stallions were leased by other ranchers for a year or two to improve the type of horses in other parts of the state.

Frank Fernald, who raised draft horses for freighting companies, ran many horses on the Diamond A Desert in northeastern Nevada. The wild horses on that range were also considered to be as fine as any raised in the valley. It was not surprising since similar bloodlines dominated both domestic and wild horses there.[12]

Farther west on ranches along the Humboldt River, near Winnemucca and south along the Sierra Nevada range, other types of stallions mixed with the wild herds. First importations of horses into western Nevada came from the Mormon settlers and were probably American horses. Later, Clydesdales and Percherons became favorites in the ranching communities of Mason and Smith valleys, and in Churchill County.

Thoroughbreds became synonymous with western Nevada through the fine stock raised by Theodore Winters on his valley ranch south of Reno. George Wingfield, a former cowboy who became part of the Goldfield mining success at the turn of the century, also raised Thoroughbreds. But "fancy horses" were a specialty on his farm, too: a result of crossing wild range mares with his Thoroughbred stallions. Wingfield also particularly prized a wild stallion caught near Winnemucca, a flashy pinto named Chino. It was considered "one of the prettiest" horses seen in the state and was used by Wingfield to breed his line of fancy horses.[13]

Other examples abound to illustrate that the horses in Nevada were of considerable variety between 1850 and World War II. And with fencing not widespread until after the Taylor Grazing Act in 1934, most of the horses and their descendants ran loose on the range for generations.

Not infrequently, escaped stallions set a pattern and standard for years in some particular part of the state. Around 1900, a black stallion shipped from the East to a Pacific Coast buyer was taken from his boxcar at Wadsworth in western Nevada for watering and feeding. His halter came loose and the horse bolted for the hills. A liberal reward was offered by the purchaser and both whites and Indians took to the hills. The search continued for some days until deemed futile. The black stallion was left to the wilds.

Years later, mustangers in the seldom-visited hills around Pyramid and Winnemucca lakes were reporting wild horses there much larger and of a better strain than had been seen previously. One handsome black stallion led to the speculation that the escaped stallion of years before had commandeered a wild band of horses and that his blood was telling on the horses being caught in that general region.[14]

Some wild herds were given proper names because of the influence of a particular stallion on the herd. A rancher named Hooker allowed his stallion to roam with wild bunches, and the Hooker strain of wild horses was an identifiable type around western Nevada.[15]

Wild Horse Canyon, south of a long-dead mining camp called Bovard, is recalled because of a Percheron stallion that once got loose around the turn of the century: a "statuesque stallion that is said would cause the eyes of Pharaoh's horses to cast a glint of green." Many attempts were made to corral the Percheron. Only his offspring fell prey to a trap corral; their Percheron sire apparently lived out his life in freedom.[16]

ii

The pattern of ranching in Nevada made it easy for horses to turn wild. It was the era of the open range: thousands of square miles of flatlands and mountains, canyons, and scores of Shangri-La valleys covered with wild rye, wheat grass, bluebunch, Indian rice grasses, and a variety of palatable forbes—and no fences.

An attitude of the early range period in Nevada looked upon raising hay as detrimental to the cattle's initiative to range and find its feed. In 1880, for example, only 520 acres of hay were cut in the entire state.[17] Horses and cattle roamed extensively. Many were never claimed during annual round-ups although cattle were searched for more diligently than some missing horses.

Periodic droughts that swept over Nevada caused many horses to be turned loose because ranches had little or no feed to sustain them. Then horses would range far for feed. Lonely for others of their kind, horses would join together and form bands.

As long as horses were loosely ranged they were constant attractions to the bands that had been wild for some years. A rancher named Wilkinson, of the 71 Ranch, turned fifteen hundred mares out on the Diamond A range to winter. The following spring when Wilkinson and his crew came to drive the mares back to the ranch, he found they had joined bands of wild horses and were virtually impossible to catch. Only a few were reclaimed.[18]

During economic slumps, horse ranchers turned out their horses—usually good stock—to be gathered at a future date. Many ran wild for the rest of their lives. When mining camps folded, or small ranchers went bust, horses not needed were turned loose.

A few mares and a stallion could increase geometrically within a few decades. There is little reason therefore to doubt that probably a hundred thousand horses were wild in Nevada by the turn of the century.[19] There were enough to warrant legislation in the 1890s to dispose of wild horses which ranchers considered predators of diminishing grass on the range.

Eastern Nevada was the greatest of wild horse ranges in the state. No matter what valley one rode through fifty years ago, wild horses abounded: all kinds, all colors. They brought forth Nevada mustangers, a hard-riding bunch of men who wore out hundreds of horses and killed a lot more—and sometimes themselves—chasing the cunning mustangs.

3

The Mustangers

Mustang fever—the itch that scratched at a man's hide—was as peculiar a passion as the one that causes men to climb mountains. A rancher's wife in eastern Nevada told me, "Once a man chases mustangs, he's nothing but a silly fool thereafter. Just a whiff of them horses in the hills, and home and chores are forgotten."

Chasing the wild horse gave full expression to the urge to hunt. Stealth, waiting for the prey, and then a breakneck chase on horseback after a fleeing mustang made the pulse pound. Part of it was the chance to capture something bigger, stronger, and fleeter than man himself. When horse ranching withered away under the impact of the motor car, and wild horses were so worthless they no longer could help pay for the mustanger's way of life, many horsemen quit the ranching lifestyle altogether, refusing to become cowpunchers. A cow outfit was just too slow paced, too drab compared to horse ranching and chasing wild ones.

For some horse runners and cowboys, the chase was the only reason to pursue the wild horse. After the horse had been roped and corralled the fever cooled and the horse was released. Indians on the Pyramid Indian Reservation today often truck their saddle horses into the nearby hills to chase and rope mustangs. Sometimes an entire day is spent seeking a herd and cutting out the stallion. Three or four Indians ride skillfully until the horse is roped, thrown, and hog-tied. The Indians relax then and talk about the merits of the chase, much as a football coach annotates the details of a successful end-run play. Afterward the horse is released to find its herd. If the capture was the first time for the stallion, the Indians speculate on how much tougher and wiser he will be the next time he is sought.

As with these Indians, for many wild horse runners in former times skillful mustanging was a high measure of a man. It required a man with courage as well as the knack to manipulate a rope and a fast horse beneath him.

Hundreds of men came to Nevada's wild horse ranges to seek both excitement and profit running horses. Some spent entire winters in the wild horse country studying the lay of the land, the routes used by the horses, and any special habits of the stallion or the herd. When spring arrived, they set their traps. More often than not the romantic notions of amateur hunters were crushed in a moment by a reality that had rarely been considered: the shrewdness of the wild horse in outwitting man-made traps and other schemes. Not infrequently a bunch of amateurs worked an entire summer with net results such as these admitted to by one such adventurer: "saddle horses worn out, grub all gone, clothes threadbare, no money, and only six or seven mares and colts caught."[1] Not a profitable summer's work, and the captured horses would be the dregs worth about eight dollars each if delivered at a railhead a hundred miles away.

Another runner remembers a summer wild horse spree that ended with nine of the saddle horses crippled and their value hardly compensated by the sale of the few captured mustangs.[2] This was one of the prices sometimes paid for mustang fever. A seasoned mustanger who wouldn't think of running his top saddle horse in a demanding stakes race would force his horse after mustangs until the saddle horse collapsed in a convulsive shudder. One rider chased a wild horse until his horse dropped. In a rage the rider jerked out his Winchester from the saddle scabbard and fired recklessly into the herd. Then he threw his arms around his dying horse and cried like a baby.[3]

As long as there are wild horses the fever persists. Five years ago on a ranch east of Carson City, a ranch manager came staggering into the ranch under the weight of saddle, blanket, and bridle. A few hours before he had ridden one of the better ranch horses into the hills across the Carson River. He saw wild horses, and like countless others before him, he gave chase. He was forgetful of all except the rope in his hand and the stallion ahead of him. He knew better, but not at the moment. He never felt when his horse was tiring under him, until the buckskin collapsed and died.

Men, too, have died chasing wild horses. Around the turn of the century in eastern Nevada, riders were hired to shoot stallions and drive the leaderless herds into bunches of tame horses held nearby. A Palomino stallion whose elusiveness earned him the name El Rio Rey was chased along with his band by a group of men riding in relays. They hoped to catch him because he was no ordinary mustang and was worth more captured alive.

The stallion was chased for nearly eighteen miles. Weaker horses in his herd dropped their tails and fell out. Finally only the stud and four other horses stayed ahead of the riders. El Rio Rey popped his tail like a defiant flag, and the mustangers knew he had reserve energy.

A rider named Hank Connors took up the last lap of the relay chase. He quickly realized he would not catch up to the stud to throw a rope on him. Since too much time had been wasted already, Connors decided to shoot the horse and do away with future temptation to chase him. He pressed the spurs into his horse for a last spurt of speed. When he was as close as he could ever expect to be, he fired a forty-four into the stallion's head. Almost at the same moment Connors' horse jumped a large sagebrush and freakishly landed both hoofs in a badger hole on the other side. Connors was propelled from his horse, and his cocked revolver went off sending a bullet into his body. He was found dead by the other riders less than a hundred yards from El Rio Rey.[4]

An expert rider and roper named Jack Keene lassoed a stallion on the run in Cortez Valley. He dallied his rope around the saddle horn to slow the stallion down. But the strain was too much for the saddle tree and it split. Keene was shot straight into the air. He landed on rocks and broke his neck.[5]

So common were falls at full gallop, and broken bones and crippling of one sort or another, that they were as casually accepted as putting one's foot in a stirrup to mount a horse.

Mustang fever had its lighter side also, and talking wild horse could be as compulsive as chasing them. Jeff Rice, who ran wild horses around Winnemucca in the 1920s, told me this story: "One Saturday night a bunch of buckaroos were in town at a brothel raising hell and putting a prop underneath. I was sitting with a mustanger named Tom. While I sipped my beer he ran off at the mouth with stories about horses he'd chased, hairbreadth escapes, and all that. He was telling me about a pinto stud he was after when one of the girls beckoned to him that it was his turn. He got up and said he'd be right back. A few minutes later he comes strolling over, throws his leg over the stool and goes on about his pinto stud as if only a comma had interrupted his story."[6]

For all the excitement inherent in wild horse chasing it was a strenuous, wasteful, and "killing" career. Good saddle horses were ruined or killed. Rarely did a specimen from the wild herds equal a well-bred saddle horse ruined in the chase. This was just one of the hard knocks and wretched disappointments mustangers endured while learning the trick of chasing wild horses.

For example, stallions that had escaped traps previously were always a puzzlement to amateur runners. These stallions had learned that men on horseback invariably chased them toward a trap, and would run in any direction other than where the men on horseback were trying to maneuver them. Professional mustangers recognized this habit of stallions that knew about traps, and would bluff them by chasing in a direction opposite from where the mustangers had laid their trap.

Successful mustangers were distinguished from tyros by the acute awareness that in chasing wild horses—"We had to use our heads because the fuzztail sure used his." It was Will James who wrote this; he and others knew the mustang to be cautious and clever as a coyote. Anyone who chased wild horses while assuming that their behavior would follow the patterns of domesticated horses, frequently failed. The stallion that evaded an amateur's attempt to capture him became even wiser and wilder. Professional runners cringed whenever they learned that a bunch of week-end mustangers were chasing horses in the country they worked.

But professional runners could be fooled by mustangs too. Walter Goldsmith, a retired saddlemaker, chased Nevada mustangs in the 1920s. His horse trapping gimmick was based on surprise. Without the surprise element, he felt, failure would always follow the mustanger. Once some friends of Goldsmith built a corral trap with fence wings extending out from the corral like a giant V, the apex being at the corral entrance.

"The trap was a dandy, all right," he said, "built in thick cedars with wings extending about a mile on each side and it would have held a herd of elephants. When a bunch of horses was started toward it they always managed to run around the edges of the trap wings. This was taken to mean the wings were too short, so some more length was added. Next time the same thing happened. This went on most of the summer."[7]

What the mustangers failed to note was that their activity constructing the corral was known by just about every horse in the area. Mustangers agree that horses will "gossip about these things," and, added Goldsmith, "two tribes of Indians couldn't force them into it."

Even seemingly trivial carelessness by mustangers could ruin days or weeks of preparation. A piece of sagebrush knocked over, too much disturbance of the brush where men had been working, a scarf or handkerchief left about—these were signs immediately noted by the horses. One mustanger reported that lightning had struck and burned a juniper close by a corral gate. "You couldn't get a mustang within a mile of it," he noted.[8] Creatures of habit, horses knew literally every inch of their range, and any irregularities were warily noted.

The corral method of trapping horses was far from efficient, but was probably better than a half dozen other schemes tried by Nevada mustangers. Some of the methods are as old as the history of wild horse chasing in the West; others were schemes devised by Nevadans, like the one attempted by an individual at Goldfield, Nevada, around 1910. He used a narcotic to catch wild horses. The plan was not without some sense.

He would fill a water trough next to a corral, and then pour a dosage of narcotic into the water. Wild horses drank the water, then became dazed and staggered about. The enterprising gentleman had only to walk up to the stupefied horses and herd them into the corral. His problem, however, was inconsistency in the amount of the dosage. Frequently it killed some of the horses, and finally it killed domestic stock that drank from the trough. After this occurred he was chased out of town.[9]

Two Salt Lake City men tried another narcotic system one year later in southern Nevada. They devised a bullet tipped with magnesium containing a gelatin capsule with a drug that opiated the horses. The magnesium dissolved in the flesh and caused no permanent injury if, that is, a vital organ was not penetrated. The complete lack of further reporting on the venture suggests the men might have been poor marksmen.[10]

Much simpler and more effective was the foot trap. It was fashioned something like a coyote trap but instead of steel jaws a loop of rope fastened around a horse's leg. A ranch foreman named G. Woods on the Chadwick and Russell Ranch near Humboldt, Nevada, apparently designed the first working model in 1911.[11] An improved variation became a stock item manufactured and sold by the Garcia Saddlery in Elko and was in common use in Nevada.[12]

In its most effective design, that trap was a small wooden box which was carefully buried on a wild horse trail, usually one going to a water hole. A loop was placed in the box and the rest of the rope was run back to a tree, a boulder, or a stake driven into the ground. A spring trigger was attached by a piece of light twine. When a horse stepped into the trap the twine snapped, releasing the trigger which caused the rope to fly up and circle the horse's leg. The moment the horse jerked back the loop tightened.

An early problem with the plan was tying the rope to an immovable object. The horse might break the rope, or its leg, or work up awful rope burns. After a while mustangers attached the rope to a log. The horse would tear up a considerable amount of scenery, said Will James, while dragging a heavy log about, but this would leave a trail to follow. A snared horse rarely dragged a log further than a few miles before becoming fatigued.

The trap did require precision setting and was sometimes more intricate in design than indicated here. More interesting than the scheme, perhaps, was how quickly horses became suspicious of something amiss on their trails. The slightest smell of man or a foreign object detoured the leading stallion or the mare he had delegated to lead. Will James told of stallions that became wise to traps on a trail, and if cattle were on the range the horse would use them as leaders. The horses waited until the cattle trailed to water and then followed behind. Mustangers countered by scattering horse droppings around the trap. Sometimes the hoof from a dead horse was imprinted away from the trap by a man crawling backwards on hands and knees. If this ruse succeeded, a curious stallion would come sniffing along the trail and step into the trap.[13] Mustangers who used this trap admit that it was a slow, tedious business and many horses got away. Still it was probably the best way to catch a stallion when a man had to work alone.

The story Joe Arthur tells in *Broken Hills* describes another sort of rope trap device. Joe had been working on the Fish Creek Ranch in eastern Nevada when two pals, Shorty and his partner Jeff, told Joe of seeing a beautiful stallion with a bunch of horses watering at a spring about a half mile from their present camp.

Shorty had his heart set on getting that stallion but was perplexed about how to go about it. The water where the horses came to drink was in a hole under an overhanging bank and the horses had to kneel to drink. Joe continues his story this way:

> Finally Shorty found a long rope and conceived the plan of putting a noose around where the horses put their heads in under the bank to drink. Then he sank a hole about five feet where he and Jeff hid to watch until the horses returned.
>
> The first night the horses were suspicious and, although thirsty, wouldn't drink; they could smell the men. They were very nervous and milled about awhile, then ran out into the open country. The second night the mares couldn't stand it any longer and came in one by one, drinking their fill, but the stallion, wild-eyed and suspicious, hung back, snorting and looking all around. Then the third night, after the mares had drunk, he came in and, not seeing anyone about, yet sensing something strange, snorted, walking around very uneasy, tossing his head and prancing about.

> At last he was so thirsty that he decided to drink, finally getting down on his knees to do so. Shorty and Jeff quickly pulled the rope tight and the noose slipped down over the stud's neck. As soon as he felt the rope he struggled to his feet, standing on his hind legs, and after giving a big snort lit out for open country just as Shorty yelled, "Stay with him, partner!"
>
> As the stallion pulled the rope tighter on his neck he became so frightened that he kept on running and dragged those two men out of the hole as if they had been shot out of a gun, the rope sliding through their hands, blistering and leaving them raw, as they went end over end. They never did see that stud again, or the rope, for that matter. Looking sheepishly at me, Shorty said, "Hell, Joe, he was a son-of-a-bitch for pullin'!"[14]

What may have been a common practice (and the least successful technique) for capturing a prize horse was called creasing or nicking. An expert marksman attempted to aim a bullet at the top of a horse's neck just in front of the withers and close to the spinal column. If exactly placed, the bullet stunned the horse into unconsciousness, allowing the shooter to hobble and halter the horse before it regained consciousness.

George Catlin, one of the first artists to venture to the West, attempted to crease a horse. According to him the technique was well known around the Red River country in Texas. Most likely creasing was discovered by buffalo hunters during an accidental shot that perfectly grazed a buffalo's neck and rendered him unconscious. The noted effect was later tried on horses.

Catlin attempted to crease an iron-grey horse with a fowling piece. Mortification and anguish, he later said, overwhelmed him when he noticed that one of the shots had broken the horse's neck, "and that he was quite dead."[15]

A keen eye and perfect understanding of a weapon's ballistics were absolutes for such a delicate shot. Most who attempted to crease a horse could only admit later that they had missed by shooting too high, or had broken the horse's neck by shooting too low.

Frank Collinson who mustanged in early day Texas candidly admitted that creasing was pure bunk. "I have tried it a great many times and have broken their necks scores of times and never caught a horse that way, and never knew of anyone that did."[16]

Collinson's estimate is probably correct although some claims have been made for successful creasing. In any case, many mustangers attempted a quick capture by creasing. Invariably, a hard-to-catch stallion fell victim to this method. Moments later (as most stories of creasing end), the mustanger stood in remorse and disgust over the dead body of the horse.

Run-of-the-mill stallions did not cause remorse. Frequently they jeopardized mustangers' success in capturing a herd in the times when many small bunches ranged close to each other. It was nearly impossible to throw the herds together for one large drive. Old-time horsemen solved the problem by shooting all the studs, except the best ones who were left to pick up the leaderless mares. When the herd was large enough, and thus more easily directed, they were run into a corral.[17]

Trapping wild horses always had the aura of rough, hell-bent-for-leather riding. It did require this; but skill, patience, and a special acumen in understanding wild horses' habits and mannerisms were even more necessary for success as a mustanger. Charles "Pete" Barnum had all the qualifications. He might just be the best of the multitudes of wild horse hunters who came to Nevada.

Barnum was in his late twenties when he arrived in about 1904. Little is known about him other than that a restless energy kept him from settling in the Dakotas where he grew up (the son of a Federal Indian Agent) and attended college.

Barnum had been a horse fancier since childhood and the news about wild horses which was emanating from Nevada was sufficiently intriguing to attract a man who welcomed challenge. The challenge: wild horses had become a locust-like plague to ranchers in Nevada's eastern and northern counties.

Wild horses were predators of precious grass in the eyes of Nevada's cattlemen, particularly in times of drought, when cattle were forced to roam farther to feed. Furthermore, when summer heat shriveled watering holes and creeks to widely separated oases, stockmen knew their cattle would have to take second turn at the water if horses and cattle arrived at the same time. This competition was not unusual as both animals tended to water at early morning or at dusk. Frequently little or no water remained for the cattle. Just as aggravating, horses were frequently guilty of trampling water holes in their cavorting. Anything that threatened cattle threatened the cattlemen. Horse breeders in Nevada had as much reason for detesting wild horses, although as horse fanciers they labored under mixed emotions. Nonetheless, a wild stallion that played havoc by raiding ranch herds grazing on the unfenced range made horse raising precarious and was not to be tolerated.

"Mormon horses," as thieving studs were called, raided a herd, cut out two or three good broodmares and lured them into joining the wild bunch. For some ranchers it was the last time they would ever see their mares again, unless it was through a binocular lens. To take chase to recover stolen mares was an expensive undertaking, in both time and money. Either extra hands were hired to chase down the missing mares, or regular hands were taken away from routine ranch work to give chase.

If a rancher ran large horse herds on the range without a stallion, he faced another aggravating problem if a wild stallion happened to steal the bell-mare — which was inevitable.

A bell-mare, a mare that wore a large cowbell strapped around her neck, kept a herd together. They would follow her, or the bell, wherever she went. Thus a mare so chosen was usually one that had been born on the range local to the ranch to which she belonged. She rarely strayed far, and neither did others of the herd.

The intriguing nature of the bell has never been completely understood, but horses, burros, and mules become as attached to the bell-mare as saints to their religious convictions. Belling a mare is an old trick. Spanish pack trains trekking through the Southwest always used a bell-mare, and mules followed her loyally on the trail. At night, after the stock was let loose to graze, the *arrieros* (packers) could sleep assured that next morning they would have only to listen for the tinkling of the bell to find the mare and the mules.

When a renegade stallion stole a bell-mare — he too was obviously intrigued by the tinkling charm — other horses attempted to follow. Ed Hanks told me that a stallion would turn savage against geldings that attempted to stick to the bell-mare — "beat hell out of 'em when they tried to follow. Without the bell-mare the rest of the herd would break off into small groups of two or three horses and go their own way."[18]

Such splintering of a large horse herd caused weeks of extra work recovering strays. Consequently, many ranchers hired "stud killers" to ride the country and kill mustang stallions that began drifting too close to ranch herds. Many stallions died this way, but there were always roaming young bachelor stallions ready to assume command of a herd that had lost its leader. The few stallion shooters might as well have shot into the sky. A more concentrated effort was needed.

In 1897, exasperated cattle and horse ranchers marched on the Legislature in Carson City with demands that legislation be passed for legalized action against the wild horses. The drafted bill was virtually the only one to cause discussion in that Legislature. Some lawmakers feared that shooting horses on the range would also take a toll of branded stock.[19] The bill was passed, however. It authorized county commissioners to grant permits to citizens of Nevada to kill wild, unbranded horses, mares, or colts, over the age of twelve months, found running at large on any government range lands of the state.[20] Shortly after, a class of men similar to those of the buffalo days saw a commercial opportunity in marketing horse hides. Shooting and skinning horses throughout the state gave promise of a new industry and a relief to ranchers. Some newspapers enthusiastically responded with the hope that Nevada would be a better place for agriculture and husbandry if every mustang was wiped off the face of the state.

Some citizens were appalled at the idea of shooting the horses. Their protests went unheeded until the entire affair backfired when hides of branded horses began appearing at an alarming rate at hide yards in Salt Lake City and Chicago. Legislators who had expressed regard for the dubious safety of tame horses had sufficient reason now to say, "I told you so."

Elko County, which had been anxious for the passage of the bill because its open cattle ranges probably had the greatest number of wild horses, suffered heavily in the loss of domesticated stock. The *Elko Weekly Independent,* in an article entitled "Horse Killing," said: "One man we know of has about $12,000 invested in fine horses. Another, over $7,000, and several with from $5,000 to $7,000. One man has colts running out that cost him forty dollars for the get, and another purchased a stallion and two mares not long ago and paid $500 for them, and they are all gone."[21]

Human nature had taken a not unpredictable course. Tame stock was much easier to approach than wild horses. A hunter might work all day just to shoot five wild ones, claim the two-dollar hides, and the manes and tails which sold for thirty cents, for a total of $11.50 for a day's work. Hunters who worked the ranges where tame horses grazed could probably shoot twenty horses much quicker and earn much more money in the same period of time.

Thus, continued the Elko paper's tirade, "branded horses are being slaughtered left and right, and the Indians' horses are being exterminated."[22]

Different complaints came from other quarters of the state. In the Pine Nut Range in western Nevada, the Raycraft Brothers, who operated a mine on the hills, echoed the protests of many when they complained about the stink coming from rotting carcasses left in the range. They had to cart away and bury carcasses of twenty horses shot almost at the doors of their cabins.[23]

Jane Riordan, whose husband ranched in Nye County, told me she could remember hearing the shooting of wild horses near her ranch house. What she hated even more was the smell that lingered for weeks and the yapping and fighting of coyotes over the carcasses night after night.[24]

Sufficient anxiety and protest had been registered over the wild horse bill of 1897 to cause an attempt at revision. In the 1899 Legislature, an assemblyman named Gedney proposed another bill, which passed the assembly but died in the senate. The bill became too complicated with assessments of branded horses on the range, which had never been accurately reported to assessors. That was incentive enough for defeating the bill.[25]

In 1901 the Legislature considered the wild horse law again. This time the legislators decided it was a bad piece of lawmaking and repealed it.[26] Presumably, without legal permits mustang hunters would be operating against the law. This was sufficient to keep hunters out, since horses running on the range technically belonged to whoever owned the range, whether the federal or county government or private owners.

Domesticated horses had taken a licking, but the wild horse herds had hardly been marred. Nor did it seem at that point that any sensible and humane scheme could be designed to rid Nevada of its wild horses. A key detriment to mustangers' efforts was the topography of Nevada which offered wild horses ideal isolation and concealment. The central and northern parts of the state are a series of north-south mountain chains. These harbor canyons and hidden valleys with often-precipitous approaches through rough juniper, cedar, and pinyon growths. Many horses learned to retreat to these recesses when chased, especially in the sparsely settled counties of Eureka, Nye, Lander, White Pine, Elko, and Humboldt. These counties comprised more than half of the state's territory and were called the last wild horse pasture in America. The horses kept to an elevation ranging from six to nine thousand feet. Bunch grass was a main sustenance during summer, and after the first frost, white sage.[27]

Seemingly, Nevada would remain a high desert stronghold which favored the wild horse rather than those who attempted their capture. Thus far, methods to harvest the herds for commercial uses had proved dismal failures.

For some time after Pete Barnum came to Nevada he worked with other mustangers to learn techniques and the mannerisms of wild horses. The wasteful procedures registered quickly in his analytical mind, especially the matter of shooting horses which he loathed as an admirer of horses. Barnum was part of that crew of riders which came upon the bodies of Hank Connors and the stallion El Rio Rey which Connors had shot moments before his own horse tripped and killed him.

Staring at the bodies, one of the riders muttered, "Poor Hank."

Barnum retorted, "Poor horse."[28]

Barnum also witnessed the shooting of another marvelous horse: a big, cunning pinto that ranged at Dry Creek on the east side of Pine Valley in Eureka County. He had escaped capture for some years, always taking his herd with him. Mustangers chased him until Barnum estimated that over two thousand dollars had been spent in various ways trying to capture the stud and his herd. Paralleling the fate of El Rio Rey, the pinto stallion was finally felled by a rifle shot. Barnum called his death a tragedy and a shame upon the human race.[29] When Barnum finally ramrodded his own crew of men, he would not allow his riders to carry guns while in pursuit of wild horses.[30]

Neither did Barnum accept the relay method of chasing horses; the waste was intolerable to his thinking. To keep a band running as riders relayed each other along a chase route usually resulted in what was known as "melting a mustang." Horses dropped dead in such extended chases. Said Barnum:

> A band closely pursued will continually lose the "tails." The innumerable canyons and gulches provide momentary hiding places . . . and a tired mare, colt, or weakling, will discontinue the race. Each rider will find when he comes within sight of them that the bunch numbers one or two less than it did previously. The poorest give out first. The greater number and best are ahead of the riders, so he disregards the individuals and continues. Perhaps the next mile another quits, soon another throws up its tail, and finally the rider may find that the bunch which numbered eighteen or twenty at the start has dwindled to two, three of four.[31]

A more efficient method that Barnum observed was the use of a *parada,* a herd of gentle horses. These would be driven to the area where mustangs were to be chased. The *parada* was left in a canyon or low spot behind a ridge to graze. A few riders would take a station close by to hold the *parada* in the general area.

Meanwhile, other riders were sweeping over the country picking up bunches of wild horses. Relay riders tended to stay out of sight as long as the horses followed the route that would lead them to the *parada.* If the wild ones started to detour, a rider showed himself just enough to cause the horses to turn back onto the chosen route.

Riders watched to see when the horses would begin to realize they were being herded; at that point the stallion would become determined to get himself and his herd away. This was a crucial moment in a chase.

If the stallion set himself a new course, followed by his herd, it might be impossible to change the stallion's direction. Barnum often rode his mount neck-to-neck with a stallion, beating it over the nose with a quirt or a rope to force it to turn. Either the stallion endured the punishment until he left the exhausted rider and horse behind him, or he suddenly slackened his pace enough to dodge behind the rider and continue his determined way.

If the chase went according to plan the wild horses were suddenly met by the *parada.* Hidden men then made themselves seen in front of the wild ones as other riders took up surrounding positions. The gentle horses mixed with the wild ones, which in theory became more tractable. By careful herding the entire herd was then moved to a holding corral.

Thousands of wild horses were caught by the *parada* system. Probably just as many were lost. A careless judgment by a rider or excessive crowding of the herd might split them into all directions. An arrogant stallion might lead the herd like a battering ram through the *parada* causing confusion and excitement, and take the *parada* right along with him. A stallion that once escaped a *parada* was almost impossible to herd again toward a group of tame horses. Consequently, as with every other system attempted, the hardiest and most intelligent horses, the best horses, continued to escape.

The corral method with its wide extending wings was the most popular among mustangers. But it also had drawbacks. The expenditure in time and effort needed to erect a corral was one. Another was that a corral had to rely on the local availability of cottonwood or juniper trees from which corral poles were cut and shaped, and the source for a corral was often many miles from where the herds ranged. Either a long chase had to be accepted, or the materials had to be hauled by wagon or pack animal closer to the herds' home range. In addition, many corrals were reinforced with woven wire or heavy cable which also had to be transported. Unless riders were skillful and worked in close unison, and knew the country and the habits of wild horses, days of work and planning might explode in a mustanger's face. Jack Grover recalls one instance after all preparations had been made:

> We scattered off to where we would pick up our "point" on the range to take up the running. Everything had been planned out the previous night before turning in. It was a rough, hard job with plenty of fast riding, hard on the horses and the men. . . .
>
> You have to pick a hiding place where the mustangs won't see you. (I have heard the scientists say that horses are shortsighted, but these scientists never ran horses on the Nevada hills.)
>
> Then, under the rays of the rising sun, you see them coming, little dots at first, then resolving themselves into miniature horses. And that was the time you had to ride. You had to keep them inside the circle and head them for the next man. He would take up the chase and run them into the next man, and so on until they were landed inside the wings of the corral. . . .
>
> More than once I have known what it was to hit camp completely alone, with a bunch of racing horses in front, get them into the wings, start crowding them and have them break back on me and scatter like beads off a broken string. Then we'd lose the whole day's work, for no outfit can hold range horses when they scatter.[32]

Even after the horses were in the corral there was no assurance they would stay. Horses were known to crash the opposite side of the corral or bounce off cable strands with a sickening crack of their legs or necks. Barnum recalled a 25 percent loss of horses in one season from this cause. One bunch of sixteen were practically annihilated when twelve of the horses were killed by headlong rushes into a woven wire fence.[33] If a gaping hole had been made in a wooden corral by the impact of some of the horses, others took advantage to flee back to the hills through the splintered opening.

The stallion—the one horse always desired—often made escape by jumping the corral and leaving his mares. A black stallion that had once made his escape in this way was again rushed into a corral with another herd he had picked up. He wasted no time. He estimated the height of the corral as he entered and never checked his speed but sped on and sailed over the barrier.[34]

Old Sontag was another stallion which refused to be held by any enclosure. This big brown stallion roamed Fish Creek Valley. He was captured a couple of times but escaped. Two years later he was caught again and placed in a field with plenty of grass and water and about sixty other horses waiting to be herded to a railhead. When the mustangers returned about ten days later to herd the horses on to their destination, the corral was completely empty. There was a gap in the heavy wire fence and the broken ends of the wire were covered with hair, flesh and blood. The mustangers readily believed that they owed their loss of sixty horses to Old Sontag. He was never seen again.[35]

Pete Barnum knew mustanging was a heartbreaking business. But he also believed that mustanging could be a profitable business venture if a better method could be developed to round up mustangs. A corral was necessary, but building one from scratch took too much time and was plain advertisement to the horses that men were in the area. And a suspicious stallion, Barnum was aware, rarely took a chance. He would take his herd in rapid exit if only a vague uneasiness indicated that man was close by.

The idea that came to Barnum's mind for quickly and efficiently capturing wild horses he credited to an inspiration. But the basis of the inspiration was his study of wild horse behavior, for he had noted that horses seldom jump or crash anything they cannot see through or over. Like most effective methods, Barnum's solution was simple. He thought of using canvas for a corral. It was light, easily portable, and could be quickly erected.

Barnum bought the heaviest and widest canvas possible and had it sewed into walls seven feet high. When unrolled it made a corral about a hundred feet in diameter. He also purchased thirty-five hundred yards of khaki-like cloth which was doubled in width and sewn together to be used as wings.

Cottonwood poles were cut, peeled, and dried. Seventeen were used for each corral. The canvas would be unrolled and stretched on the outside of the poles, which would lean slightly inward, and when the poles were guyed tightly from the outside the canvas would stretch drum tight.

The walls and wings were cut into sections, each section to be portaged by a pack animal. Two corrals were joined together as a figure eight. The back corral would serve as a holding corral and allow the gate of the front corral to be kept open for additional herds to be run in. The idea of moving a corral which could be erected swiftly had been solved. Next was the testing of the scheme. Barnum has described that first experiment:

> It was late November when all was ready. Although it was too late in the season to do much, we were anxious to try the corrals, so prepared for a short trip to the mountains. Pole Creek, the name given to a section of range about thirty miles south of Palisade on the west side of Pine Valley [Eureka County], was chosen as the best place for the experiment. Saddle horses, forty-six in number, and already nearly worn out with work, were again gathered. Six pack horses were also selected for their share of the work, but we had to enlist the services of four more pack horses, for although we successfully packed corrals, poles and camp outfit upon the chosen six, every animal lay down. Although I asked them politely, and later used persuasion of a more decided character, they refused absolutely to get up, so we had to remove the packs, divide the loads among four more horses, and found that they all had enough even then. We started about noon. That night we camped in the mountains ten miles south. Soon after sunrise the following morning we were ready to start, and by a little urging we reached our destination shortly after dark that night. During our drive from Palisade to this point we were seldom out of sight of wild horses, which were very inquisitive for they had been undisturbed for a

long time. I could recognize none of the leaders, but their numbers promised much and made us even more eager to try the corrals. We had decided to erect them on a ridge which we had learned was a favorite one for them to use in going from the mountains to the flat below, so with all possible haste and with very little noise we set the poles and stretched the canvas, being somewhat disappointed in finding that it took the greater part of the day to accomplish this.

There were four men beside myself: Dicey, a full-blooded Shoshone Indian, Miguel Quiroz, Chico, and Bascus, three Mexican vaqueros possessed of good judgment and plenty of experience. Before starting out the next morning I again explained to them that much depended upon the success of our undertaking, that I expected every man to ride through blazes if necessary to corral these horses, and hinted that any lukewarm performances would be noticed by me and dealt with accordingly.

Miguel and Chico left early and rode north about two and a half miles, climbing to the crest of a mountain in their endeavor to get around a band which they discovered soon after leaving camp. They were successful in getting to their desired position and started fourteen head on a run toward the wings of the corral. For some reason unknown to us the leader turned east toward the flat immediately, completely ignoring the ridge we expected they would strive to use for this purpose. I had stationed myself about half a mile north of the end of the wing nearest the horses. Perceiving the intention of the leader I tried to ride in front and below them so as to cause them to take a southerly course along the side of the mountain until they were inside the wings of the corral. In this I was unsuccessful, they being determined to keep the course they had started upon.

Seeing that it was useless to try to hold them above or even level with the end of the wing, I quickly worked my way above them, with the idea of allowing them to go below the corrals, hoping that we might be able to turn them back to the mountains and then into the wings after they had reached a point high enough and suitable for this purpose. Miguel and Chico understood my new move, and without orders rode in the manner they deemed best. Both rode at breakneck speed directly down the side of the mountain, knowing that about a half a mile below was a pass that the leader was striving to use in his effort to get his band to the flat country to the east. To get there first would cause the mustangs to turn south, which would eventually lead them back to the mouth of our corrals. The movement called for quick work and hard riding, but all knew that the time to outrun a wild horse is to do it down hill—for if you cannot beat him down hill, you surely cannot do it going up. Quirt and spur were not spared, and we gained our point.

Miguel, Chico and myself were below these wild horses and running as fast as the leaders, and they gradually turned from us toward the mountains above. The horses carrying the Mexicans were badly distressed, having been running as fast and a little farther than the wild ones and carrying about two hundred and thirty pounds of man and rigging, so believing that I would be able to handle the band until relieved, they returned to camp for fresh horses. My horse, though somewhat winded, still had plenty of go in him.

Twice I dismounted and led him up two of the steepest ridges, which gave him a chance to recover somewhat, and by forcing him down the slopes I was able to influence the course of the band toward a point which, if I could maintain my speed, I knew would bring us just inside the wings. It was a long, hard race. The sagebrush was very thick and high, my horse jumped much of it instead of going around. This, together with the fact that we had to cross many washes and ditches and were constantly climbing the mountains drew heavily on his reserve strength. Inwardly I was losing hope. The wild horses were running very strong, all staying close to the leader and only a few suckling colts being very far behind.

> Just then out from behind a rocky ridge rode Dicey, the Indian, with a yell and a dash that was a credit to his race, straight for the leader. Over rocks and badger holes down the side of a mountain that would cause a man to exercise care afoot, this daredevil Indian rode at race-horse speed until he was just ahead of the big bay stallion in the lead. The stud saw and heard him and turned away from him. I knew now that we had a chance to win, so closed in behind and to the right of the band. At the same time I saw Miguel appear in the distance to the left of the mustangs and just beyond him were Chico and Bascus. The horses were now within the wings of the corral and five men were behind them. The leader had noticed the wings to the right and left and was acting as if he would turn back. We knew he was likely to do so when he saw the corrals directly ahead of him, so bent every energy to the task of crowding them in. They were running slower now, some dodging from one side to the other in a confused sort of way. Yelling and beating the air with quirt and rope we literally forced them through the gate. They were corralled.[36]

The corral proved itself completely effective. What was to become routine for thousands of horses chased by Barnum and his crews was observed here once the horses were corralled. They circled about in a quandary, some running in one direction while others skirted the canvas enclosure from the other direction. But none tried to run against it. Stallions would frequently kick savagely against it with harm neither to themselves nor the canvas. Plenty of time was allowed for the horses to settle into a quiet, submissive mood in their confinement. Then the gate at the far end of the corral was opened and the wild ones urged into the second corral, which held some gentle horses. The canvas gate flap was shut behind them. The front gate of the first corral was opened ready to receive another band.

Barnum's canvas corral revolutionized the mode of capturing wild horses. Now range country that had proven havens for the mustangs because no timber was available for corrals was accessible to Barnum.

By next season he had several traps, each under separate crews, working the wild horse ranges throughout four counties of eastern Nevada. Anywhere from ten to thirty head could be caught at one run with two or possibly three such runs a day. With an experienced crew the corral could be erected in two hours and was best assembled under cover of darkness. The chase commenced at first light. In this way the horses were kept ignorant of the trap. Many herds ran blindly into the corral before they became aware of their predicament.

Barnum also used the terrain to advantage to accelerate "first run catches." Horses are much like cows in that they follow definite trails or runs. A bird's eye view of the rolling desert hills in Barnum's time would reveal dust-beaten paths that wound their way to water holes, over passes, and through dry washes. These natural runways were carefully considered when erecting the canvas corral. If the horses were not excessively pushed during a chase they could be relied upon to follow their trails.

Since many trails followed ridges which gave the horse visual advantages, traps were set about a hundred yards off the trail or down on the side of a ridge. When the horses attempted to cross from one ridge to another they plunged unknowingly into the earth-colored canvas.

Barnum's canvas trap insured a higher percentage of captured horses. Still, the exhausting runs, the crippling or killing of good saddle horses, and the prevalent danger to the riders remained constant. Whenever possible, therefore, the safer practice of trapping horses at a water hole was exercised. Mostly this procedure involved patient waiting.

Water hole trapping was not used as much in the northern parts of the state as in the central and southern areas. Where water was prevalent any suspicious man-smell caused the horses to seek another place to drink. If, however, not many watering places were available mustangers might place "spooks," sometimes called "ghosts," around all the water holes except one.

Spooks were nothing more than brush, rags, or anything else that would spook the horses away from that particular watering place until the thirsty mustangs finally turned to the only one available, where a trap awaited them.

In the arid regions of the state, water holes might lie twenty to fifty miles apart, forcing horses to enter a trap which surrounded an oasis. Rarely was any concealment of the trap attempted. They stood stark on the open, flat desert.

Mustangs watered, depending on how far they had to travel to a water hole, anywhere from every twelve to every twenty-four hours. Dusk and early morning were their usual times, and if not disturbed the herds would always drink from the same water hole.

A trap would be erected in early spring around an oasis. A smaller holding corral would be built onto the main corral. After being erected the gates from both the main corral and the smaller one would be opened and secured, so the horses might walk freely through. The mustangers would then depart the area.

At first sight of the corrals surrounding the water hole the horses would stampede away. They would travel to another place to drink, but men would already have been there and spooked that water hole. Suspicion kept the horses from the opened corral until intense thirst finally forced some to enter and drink. As nothing happened, they rapidly accepted the presence of the corral and soon wandered unconcerned in and out of it.

A few weeks later the mustangers would return. They would hide themselves in holes previously dug close by the main gate, called "nests," which were large enough to be fairly comfortable. A hole-cover of logs or brush slid over the top to conceal the mustangers. Hours would be passed in the nests while waiting for the first herd to appear.

Soon after dusk the faint pounding of hoof beats on the hard desert floor would emerge out of the stillness. The mustangers would remain still until the horses had filed past them into the corral and were drinking. Then they would leap from the nest and secure the gate. This was no simple trick. During Barnum's time closing the gate required hard manual effort, a rush to slam the gate shut and secure it before the sudden appearance of man forced a desperate rush by the horses. There was risk involved. Of course the horses might rush toward the back of the corral, which was a relief to the mustanger. But what happened to a mustanger named Frank Hale was possible with any man who worked a water trap in this fashion.

Hale had a water trap at Barrel Springs in Newark Valley, White Pine County. After a herd had entered the corral, Hale rushed out of his hiding nest to close the gate. The stallion had been the last to enter and was close by. The moment he saw Hale darting toward the corral the stud sprang from a leap and hit the gate just as Hale was swinging it shut. It hit Hale full force knocking him down, and wrenching the gate from its hinges. The herd stampeded through the opening and crushed Hale to death.[37] (Eventually a spring and lever technique was developed which allowed the gate to be slammed shut without mustangers leaving the nest.)

Once the horses were trapped they were spooked into the holding corral. The main gate was again propped open, and the men retreated to their nests to await another herd.

The number of horses that might water in one evening could be more than the traps would hold. Barnum, in 1906, returned to a trap he had built in 1905 to estimate how many horses might be caught at that particular spring. He spent a night, starting about seven o'clock one evening and staying until dawn the next morning. A hundred and twenty head of horses, including foals, passed through the corral to water. This was an exceptional number, probably twice the usual number, Barnum admitted. It did prove that the spring was the only water for many miles around and a prime trapping area.[38]

A mustanger who worked alone to capture a stallion, or a

fine domesticated horse that had turned wild, found easy success roping the horse after it had drunk. Sometimes a rider would strip his horse of its saddle weight and tie one end of his rope around the horse's neck. Then he waited in hiding or upwind from the mustang's approach to the water hole.

After the wild ones had drunk their fill of water the mustanger, riding bareback, would spur his horse from hiding and into the herd. If lucky, he might make his catch immediately before the mustang could gain speed. Usually a chase ensued, but now the advantage was with the rider since a waterlogged horse had no capacity for sustained speed. Normally a quarter of a mile was all a mustang could endure before the rider caught up with him and circled a rope over the wild one's head.

The rider hauled back on the rope, slowly cutting off the wind of the wild horse, until exhaustion tumbled the mustang. Sometimes a rider was a bit more fancy. He would throw the slack in his rope over the mustang's quarters and hind legs and then turn his own horse away at a right angle and trip the mustang. Busted in this manner and filled with water, the horse was quickly tied hind and front and left secured. Mounting again, the mustanger took chase after other horses of the herd. A good man on a good horse could catch four or five mustangs in this way, and a legion of men believed that the best trap was a fast horse and a long rope.

ii

Wild horses in a corral afforded the mustanger no assurance of permanent capture, just as a marlin fighting on a line would not be the property of an angler until it was lying on deck.

Moving captured horses to a railhead at Eureka, Beowawe, or Palisade required a march of ten to fifty miles depending on how far south of the Central Pacific Railroad Barnum and his riders had caught their horses. And just as losing a prize marlin after hours of struggling effort was disheartening, so was the loss of herds that had required days to corral. Mustangers took no chances on the long drive to the railhead, and the methods used to keep herds from stampeding were as ugly as they were effective.

One way was to wire a horse's nostrils together. No breath, no running. Another was to cut a small ligament on the front leg and let the joint-water drip out. This method stiffened the front legs and one mustanger could safely herd a large band of horses.

Neither of these techniques was prevalent in Nevada, but cruelty is relative. Most Nevada mustangers had no qualms about tying a rope tightly around a horse's hind leg above the hock and over the hamstring. Horses were then forced to walk in a crippled limp.

Indian mustangers favored nailing heavy tar paper or shingles to a horse's hoof. The horse would then have to assume a tiring, high-stepping walk or else trip itself.

Probably the commonest practice was to tie a rope from the tail to the head, just short enough to hold the horse's head turned in toward its body. This method also kept the horse to a walk.

The whip chain was another favorite. A two-foot chain hooked to a piece of leather was wrapped around the front legs just above the hoof. The horse had perfect freedom of movement as long as it stayed at a walk or easy trot. A faster gait caused the chain to begin whipping and stinging about the legs, which quickly brought the horse back to a walk.

This formula was the most humane but apparently wasn't known in Barnum's time. His method was to lasso and throw a horse and tie a front leg up against the elbow. A drive commenced with the horses hopping on three legs.

"The going is painful," said Barnum, "and their stubborn spirit or resistance is broken down. Presently a horse grows weary and lags behind. This is the sign that he surrenders. We rope and throw him, remove the rope that binds up his foreleg—and find that we can now drive him along without difficulty. If the spirit of rebellion rises again the horse is given another treatment."[39]

Most of Barnum's horses satisfied demands for cheap work horses on farms in the Midwest and the South, and in cities where wagon transportation was reaching its peak. San Francisco was a constant market for cable car horses, whose span of usefulness was about two years because hard-top roads rapidly weakened a horse's legs. Agents from St. Louis, Salt Lake City, and Kansas City kept standing orders for Barnum's Nevada wild horses. In winter months Barnum kept the better horses to break on his ranch south of Eureka. These sold for fifty to a hundred dollars each. Unbroken mustangs peddled for ten dollars and were usually sold by the carloads. Mediocre and aged horses went to a rendering plant at Petaluma for conversion to chicken feed.

Barnum kept the finest horses—and there were many running in his time—either for training or as breeding stallions. Some of these better horses sold for as high as seven hundred dollars.[40]

Barnum's fifteen-year sojourn in Nevada witnessed the removal of about fifteen thousand wild horses. It is a phenomenal figure for him and his men. Mexicans, Indians, and whites did it all the hard way, on horseback.

No one knows how many other horses left the state by way of other mustangers who engaged in the wild horse business. It was not an uncommon occupation in Nevada. Signs or notices in newspapers of the period record many who dealt in wild horses:

WILD HORSES FOR SALE

> Anyone interested in the purchase of wild horses can be supplied with a number of these animals. For further particulars address P.O. Box 72, Eureka, Nevada.[41]

Barnum became king of the wild horse catchers, and he rode during the final crest of man's need for horses. But soon after, except for the demand caused by World War I, they became anachronisms, and so did the men who chased them. In 1914, virtually Barnum's last recorded remark was, "What breeds was it they crossed to produce this automobile hybrid anyway?"[42]

Barnum retired from what he called the "truest sport and finest business in the world." He saw that the horse would be a relic in the years ahead. And if horses were no longer to be used for what they were intended, he wanted nothing to do with catching them only for chicken feeders and pet food manufacturers. To so use aged and poor horses was one thing. But to watch young, well-proportioned, beautiful horses taking the same route was more than he could tolerate. When he quit, he reflected the attitude of many horse-living, horse-loving buckaroos who would not be part of "grinding up horses." Barnum went East and was never heard of again.

"Give the horse a little consideration," said one old horseman, "and being he has to go, let him vanish in the country he belongs in. A little bullet back of the ear would eliminate the long runs into the traps, the lockjaw that's caused from the runs, the little colts that are left behind to mope around and die, the broken necks in hitting the traps, the broken legs, and broken hearts, and so on."[43]

Of course that wasn't an easy way out for the horses either. Besides, there was still money to be made from the wild horses. Men in airplanes showed a new way to capture the wild ones. Later they joined with men in flatbed trucks and they were no longer horsemen, but dispassionate businessmen.

4

The Stallion and His Herd

Mustangers—successful mustangers—owed their prowess to an understanding of wild horse behavior. Attaining that skill meant never expecting tame horse behavior from a wild horse. The wild stallion, especially, mustangers agreed, was an extraordinary creature. To liken him to a domestic horse would be as misleading as comparing a zoo-raised lion to its African plains counterpart.

Perhaps stemming from jealous possessiveness of his mare herd, a wild stallion could be a vicious fighter. If he should attack a man, perhaps become a "killer hoss," or outlaw, he was about the most dangerous animal next to a grizzly that could be encountered.

Herman Smoot, who ran wild horses in the hills outside

Carson City in the 1920s, told me a rider had to be careful approaching wild herds. "You never knew for sure about the stud. Sometimes when he saw you coming he would lay his ears back and charge up to you, maybe fifty feet or so just to bluff you while his mares took off. That was one type. He then usually turned right around and followed after them.

"I've seen others, they're rare, leave their herd and trot up to you like some friendly horse wanting its nose rubbed. Then, when they were close enough, they'd explode in a lunge that stopped your heart. My God! You don't know fright until you have a stud towering over you with hooves and a gaping mouth almost big enough to swallow you."

Another time Smoot drove a captured herd to a corral at the Nevada State Prison at Carson City. The stud leader was mean and fought Smoot and some inmates when any attempt was made to separate him from his mares. One morning Smoot tried again to drive the stallion into a separate corral. Suddenly the horse rushed Smoot and knocked him into a feed manger. "He was ready to eat me, and would have if I hadn't flayed like hell with my legs.

"Some of the prison boys later tried to ride him, but he bit their legs and ripped off their overalls. I finally gave him to a vaquero. But the stud got away and went back to the hills."[1]

It was not always possible to tell an outlaw stallion. A rider watched his saddle horse for a cue: a twitching of the horse's ears or a nervous acting-up could mean dangerous intent from a wild stud. Phillip Ashton Rollins wrote in *The Cowboy* that one horse in five hundred was an outlaw and could never be broken, and one in ten thousand was a man-killer.[2] Rollins's last estimate is probably wide of the true mark. A number of mustangers have told me stories similar to Smoot's, and have added: "We took no chances. We'd shoot a stud if it started coming at us like a pet dog."

Seemingly, some studs are ready to attack whatever appears as a threat. Wendell Wheat, a trapper from Fallon,

Nevada, and a keen observer of wild things, told me he was driving his pickup truck on one of the back roads of Brunswick Canyon near Carson City when a wild stallion leaped out from behind a boulder.

"That stud eyed my truck like it was a lion. He arched his neck and pranced in place like he dared me to come an inch closer. If he'd started to attack the truck with his hooves, and I had the feeling he would, I might have a long walk ahead of me. I just backed the truck away. Most unusual action I've ever seen in a wild horse."

Curious, too, how strongly the wild nature persists in domesticated stock: for some, only a slight incentive carries them back to primitive herd instincts.

The Hunter and Banks Cattle Company near Elko, Nevada, once turned out a black Percheron stallion to run with a herd of ranch mares. Soon miners in the area complained of being chased by a mean black stallion. A rider named Ed Hanks and another called Lester were sent to "tame" the stud.

Ed lassoed the stallion. "He was as gentle as a kitten," said Hanks, although he noticed his own horse seemed sort of nervous.

"Lester," said Ed, "we can't whip this horse or tame him because he hasn't done nothin' very much this morning."

"No, I think he's already tame," Lester replied.

The stud was turned loose. He returned to his mares and started to leave the area. Ed galloped after them to turn them back the other way when his horse stumbled. Ed was busy for that second trying to help his horse recover when Lester yelled, "Look out!"

Ed looked around "into blazing eyes, just in time to yank my leg away from the wicked teeth of the black stallion. He clenched his teeth on the skirt of my saddle where my leg had been, and pulled back, tearing several long gashes in my new Walker saddle."

Ed got away, but that "tame" stallion finally had to be taken off the range.[3]

What knowledge we have of wild horse behavior comes from those who chased and lived with wild horses. Although they were students of wild horse behavior as any hunter must be of his quarry, they lacked a scientific method. They made prolific but often contradictory observations.

The stallion, for example, is recognized as the leader, yet he has often been observed following a herd while an aged mare takes the lead. In Texas, John Young in the *Vaquero of the Brush Country* told his biographer, J. Frank Dobie, how rope snares were placed across trails as capturing devices: "The mustang that was snared was usually a stallion leading his *manada* [herd]."[4]

Will James worked the same technique but generally caught an old mare, "the leader of the bunch."[5]

James chased horses in Nevada's desert hills; Young on the Texas brush range. Both observations are accurate but neither explains "leading" behavior. Nor is this easy to do with a number of other wild horse ways.

It is particularly difficult if one is talking about horses that were once domesticated and later went wild. These *cimarrones* are known to be more clever from their association with man. They become the wildest and craftiest of any wild bunch they join.

Will Barnes, a dedicated early-day forester who knew range land and range stock, wrote: "It is a well-known fact that the hardest to 'cut-out,' the leader of them all in a race across the prairie, is the old, gentle, well-broken saddle or work horse once he gets a taste of freedom."[6]

James Cook, an Indian scout in his youth on the western frontier, said about the same thing: "Strange as it may seem, the well-broken gentle horses and mules which joined the band of mustangs and lived with them for a few months or years, became, if such a thing could be, more wild and watchful than the mustangs."[7]

No wonder Nevada's wild horses, many of which were formerly domesticated, were considered more difficult to catch than those on other western wild horse ranges. Archie Dewar, born and raised in Elko, Nevada, and now in his eighties, grew up hearing about the Murphy horses, two saddle horses that "went with the wild bunch" on Elko Mountain. Both horses were geldings, about five or seven years old when they went wild. For twenty years they evaded capture. Archie tells it this way:

> The Murphy horses got loose about 1889 or 1890. They spoiled more good horses that happened to get loose and join them than a parcel of bad cowboys. If you lost a horse, and it joined the Murphy horses, you just about gave up on ever getting it back.
>
> The Murphy horses were always on the lookout—one always standing on the alert. Just the sight of a man coming near their area and the animal would give a whistle, an alarm system that put every horse on the alert. If chased, they would split, each taking a part of the herd with them. It was tough enough trying to run down horses through the brush, but when they split it made chasing almost worthless. They knew every effort that cowboys might attempt in a chase.

For twenty years no one was able to capture them. I never could understand why they weren't shot, but they were finally killed by two cowboys who caught them while they were looking for a lost buggy horse.[8]

Although the horse is a habit-loving animal he is flexible enough in the wild state to make one cautious in ascribing specific practices to him. In spite of some contradictions, however, observations of many mustangers have established certain patterns of wild horse behavior.

ii

The stallion, like most leaders, sets the mold. He dominates a herd, band, bunch, drove, or, in the Southwest, a *manada*. The size of his herd depends on what he is able to fight for and defend. Most reports indicate eight to ten mares to one stallion. Twenty is another figure often stated, and even fifty mares have been observed under command of a single stallion. A prairie environment undoubtedly allowed a larger herd than did Nevada's arid, broken landscape. In the early days when they had more room to roam, Nevada stallions had from a dozen to twenty-five mares. Today the herd size appears to average from ten to fifteen mares.[9]

As with most grazing animals the horse is gregarious, and herd life is a protection against predators. A lone horse is a miserable creature who tends to become nervous and develop anxiety habits. Mustangers have reported a lone wild horse joining their bunch of tame horses out of pure loneliness for his kind. If he could not find security and companionship with other horses he might join up with a herd of elk, antelope, or buffalo.

The individual is far safer eating and resting in a herd while another member serves as a sentinel. Usually the stallion is on guard, sometimes from a high piece of terrain where he can observe from a distance and keep tabs on what the winds carry. Both his sight and smell are acute, probably far better than a dog's, and men or predators following the wind will be detected long before they know themselves that wild horses are in the vicinity.

Some mustangers believe the type of country determines a stallion's technique of guard duty. Broken, mountainous terrain that diminishes the range of his visual and olfactory senses will lead him to seek a prominent height allowing full command of sight and sound. On open prairie where a stallion can see and smell as far as the winds can blow, he grazes away from the herd, but constantly circles about. He nibbles a few bits of grass, lifts his head to observe and take a whiff of the air, then lowers his head for another bite.

His periods of rest do not leave the herd unguarded. The responsibility is delegated to an aged mare who, in the order of rank, is next in command. Her special role in the herd is mentioned later.

During rest periods and sleep, rarely do all horses lie down together. One animal is on the lookout, even though it may appear asleep, and it reacts to the slightest disturbance.[10]

Communication is subtle and varied. Probably the rarest utterance to be heard is a stallion's whistle, a sharp, loud blowing breath through the nostrils. It carries a great distance and is the stallion's warning of immediate danger. It is rarely heard among domesticated horses.

The more familiar neigh is probably a distress call and is frequently heard when horses are separated or when feeding time is approaching. A nicker, a soft, rattling breath utterance, seems to be an expression of pleasure or relief. Mustangers made a point of listening to "hoss talk" to gauge the mood of a herd.

Visual signals among horses also were closely watched. Even slight movements of the tail, a certain cocking of the ears, or a muscular twitch of the lips and nose, conveyed meaning. Mustangers, hidden at a watering hole, watched a leader bringing a herd to drink. Usually a herd approached single file and the leader would convey signals to be passed back as to whether a line should halt or wait while the leader checked for danger at the watering place.

Unlike other hoofed animals the wild stallion maintains constant ownership of his herd of mares. Bison, some deer, elk, and antelope separate until rutting season, when adult males gather females for temporary, but exclusive, ownership.

Moreover the wild stallion is a despot who tolerates no threat to his supremacy as a herd leader. Young stallions beginning to display attention to mares are ruthlessly driven from the herd. He is the most polygamous and militant ruler in the mammal world. And he can fight.

Harry E. Webb, who ranched and chased wild horses in the Elko cattle regions before World War I, told me this story:

I once turned a big stud out with a bunch of mares. A couple of days later I saw the mares, but not the stud. I supposed he'd taken up with another bunch—which didn't matter too much as most of my horses and those of other ranchers were easily corralled.

A few days later a Basque sheepherder told me he had witnessed a stallion fight. "They fight all day," he said, "right near my camp."

Some days later a sorry looking critter I didn't recognize limped down the road and turned into the lane. It was my once-beautiful stud. His neck, throat, and head were a puffed mass of dry, curled skin. His head hung to the ground, swinging like a pendulum, and his left knee was disjointed. Most of his ribs were broken, and he had lost half his former weight. A mustang stud had reduced him to chicken feed.[11]

Years ago when large horses were wanted to haul wagons and heavy freight, ranchers turned out quality draft stallions to breed size into the wild herds. Sometimes the following happened.

Herman Smoot turned out a Percheron stallion, a giant-sized work horse, in the Pine Nut Hills near Carson City. A few days later the stallion returned to the ranch, chased out by a wild stud. "We knew that a stallion turned out might have to fight for a herd, and usually he could hold his own against a small wild stud. After all, just one knock from a Percheron's hoof is enough to make any horse leave the country. So, I turned the Percheron loose again, and again he was sent back home, beaten. I couldn't get him to leave the corral area after that."[12]

A wild stallion fight was the great drama of the range to mustangers. To observe stallions in poses of challenge was, they say, an electrifying sight. Every nerve of the stallions is alert, and they prance with fantastic lightness as they spar with each other. Heads are held high and tails arch straight up, like a flagpole, with the tail hair a pluming banner that signals an impending struggle.

Mares of a challenged leader tend to bunch, sensing they are the prize, although they are indifferent to the outcome of a struggle between stallions. If they do not bunch, the herd leader will force them into a tight group before he meets the intruder.

Apparently not all challenges end in battle. There is first a prelude, a display of belligerence through a ritualistic series of feints, struttings, and vocal challenges as the opponents size up each other. Bluffing, too, enters as a tactic when one stallion turns and looks askance at the warlike display of the opponent. If the intruder senses he is overmatched, he departs. Otherwise excitement erupts into a powerful onslaught.

For his size and weight the horse is agile. His hooves, stone hard, strike and kick with whiplash speed. His teeth rip hide and muscle. Combatants rear and paw, drop to their knees as each attempts to get a vice grip with his teeth on a hock or tendon, or rush alongside each other parrying for a tooth hold on the neck or withers.

One old-time vaquero said that a biting horse will kill one that attacks by kicking. If a biter can take a firm hold on the neck or withers of his opponent, he will hold on until the other is dead.[13]

Stallions can tear up a lot of country as well as themselves if evenly matched. They may fight for hours. The stallion that has successfully defended his right to a herd and his territory is rarely the pretty, unblemished sight moving pictures depict.

"Any stud that has been worth his hide," a horse-runner told me, "is tattooed with scars. You can read his history from scars, patches of white hair (deep wounds after healing often grow white hairs), a knocked down hip or an ear bitten off, just as sure as a cowhide can tell you where it has been from the brands."[14]

Age, of course, plays its crucial part in a fight between stallions. An aged herd leader pitted against a vigorous four- or five-year-old challenger might hold his own at first, but the younger stallion will continue to provoke a fight until he has won. A beaten leader might try to regain his mares, usually unsuccessfully. The winner gains strength and confidence in his newly-won pride and is difficult to lick. An aged and beaten stallion will wander away. He might attempt to fight a younger, weaker stallion, if only to claim one mare by stealing her. If he is truly old, however, past fifteen and losing the urge that gives him importance, he'll probably wander along, join up with bachelor studs or die shortly after.

Studies by naturalists indicate that a rivalry fight between male animals is not a fight to the death, but only to make a rival depart. Death occurs only rarely to one of the combatants. Wolves, for example, fight desperately, but when the loser realizes the hopelessness of his position he bares his throat to the defiant winner. But a "wolf code" keeps a victor from taking the offering.

Apparently once the fighting opponents know how the fight will end, the weaker one leaves. Bull elk, male seals, and other sexually aggressive mammals seem to confirm this theory. One animal behaviorist, while eschewing anthropomorphism, believes that although animals have much pride they will not die for it. Says this naturalist: "Killing in this situation would not be according to nature's program. Nature is always concerned for the future of the species, and those vanquished bulls, bucks, rams, cocks, and other males still will be needed to father young."[15]

Mustangers' descriptions of stallion fights are at odds with that theory, however. John Young of Texas said that a fight to the death was not unusual, and the crippling of one or both horses was common.[16]

A perceptive horseman named William Tevis, who wrote a little treatise on the horse in 1922, witnessed a stallion fight on a desolate alkali waste between Rattlesnake Mountain and the Carson Sink. Two stallions, leaders of rival bands, were engaged in a battle: "With screams of rage and ripping teeth they fought until one, gashed in the throat, was left convulsed in its death struggles on the alkali waste that it had long called its own."[17]

Another cause of fighting besides sexual rivalry could be the concept of territory, a claim to a piece of private domain. Possibly protection of territory is the basic impulse to combat between stallions, or perhaps territorial and sexual possessiveness are interwoven.

No one really knows. But despite the poetic fantasy that portrays the wild horse as a roaming, free-willed spirit of the Western plains, he seems to be inclined toward the confines of a home range more than to gypsy wanderings. "Home Range" is the term used by mustangers and ranchers to refer to the horse's territory.

Territorial concepts have only recently come into focus. Zurich's eminent animal psychologist, H. Hediger, has proposed the thesis that territoriality is the frame in which propagation is insured and which regulates density. It coordinates the group's particular habits and activities, insures group safety and keeps the species within communicating distance of each other.[18]

Marston Bates, another expert, says that territory is "usually defended against intrusion by other members of the same species, and is perhaps the commonest cause of intraspecific fighting among animals."[19]

Territorial boundaries depend on the size of the animal and the sort of existence its nature prescribes. A grazing animal would, it seems, have a flexible boundary, whereas animals that create nests would be confined to their immediate areas.

Horses are believed to be territorially oriented. Mustangers have used the term "home range" inclusively, and mean something different from what scientists have defined as territory. Home range is an extensive area where one or more herds may graze. It is shared and is not the exclusive property of one stallion. Territory is the private area of a particular stallion and his herd, and it may not be entered by another stallion or other horse without there being a challenge. While mustangers to whom I have spoken recognize these behavioral traits in horses they have tended to gather them under the idea of a horse's home range. All definitions take on the feeling of a home area, however, in what horsemen in the Southwest call *querencia*, a Spanish word that conveys the feeling of a home range as the haunt for heart and spirit.

Not even when being chased will horses leave the confines of their home range, which might extend fifteen or twenty miles. Mustangers knew this; when erecting traps and planning the pattern of a horse chase, they took into account the horse's tendency to circle back. Even after horses were captured and moved miles from their home range, care had to be taken that the horses did not attempt to return. The homing instinct is apparently strong in horses, and some have been known to travel considerable distances to return to their home range.

Joe Clifford, who owns Stone Cabin Ranch near Tonopah, told me of one of his horses, which was stolen by a sheepherder some years ago and later was found and identified by the Las Vegas sheriff. Joe wrote and told the sheriff to turn the horse loose. It arrived at the ranch three days later, after having traveled about 190 miles over desert and mountains.

Will James knew of some range horses, taken away at an early age, that came back to their home grounds to die, years later.[20] And Lee Rice, back in 1911, helped herd a hundred Nevada mustang mares to his father's ranch on the King's River in California to breed to a German Coach stallion. The mares were turned loose on a large unfenced pasture. "It didn't work," Lee told me. "Those Nevada mustangs got homesick for the open sagebrush country. We had to ride almost day and night, trying to hold them. Two bunches even reached the San Joaquin River, twenty miles away, trying to return to their Nevada range. Two weeks of this and we and our horses were rode to a frazzle. All the mares on the range were trailed back to the ranch and kept, at extra expense, under fence."[21]

An indication that the stallion, at least, is territorially oriented is his manner of driving young stallions from his herd. A stud leader becomes savage when he drives young males out of the herd and will kick and bite at them while driving them off. The bachelor stallions hang about for days at a certain distance from the herd which, apparently, is the invisible periphery of the territory's boundary. Some of the outcasts whinny with anxiety and try to close the distance between themselves and the herd. But when they have encroached a certain distance the herd stallion attacks again until the colts have retreated, presumably beyond the territorial limit.

Similar behavior has been observed when a herd stallion is approached by another stallion looking for a herd of its own. Both stallions observe each other from a distance. The herd stallion will go through aggressive motions although a fight will not occur unless the challenger has crossed over into the territorial domain of the herdmaster.

Ed Hanks, now retired in Fallon and with many memories of horse ranching days in northern Nevada, tends to believe in the territorial exclusiveness of a stallion. On one of the ranches he worked, it was a practice to run in many bunches of wild herds, turn the studs loose, and then select mares and young stuff to be broken and sold. Hanks said:

> The studs cavorted on a rise of ground about a quarter of a mile away. When we finally turned out the mixed bunches of mares, the stallions raced down the hill and rammed into the mare herd. Each stallion cut out his own mares. It was amazing to watch them. There was a lot of squealing and nipping and momentary encounters when stallions ran into each other. In a short time each stud had his own mares packed into a cluster while he paraded around his bunch. All the studs set up a considerable distance from each other, parading about until the idea got around that no other stud was attempting to claim more than his share. I'm sure that if any stud attempted to approach within fifty feet of another herd, he would have had to fight. Eventually, they settled down and drifted their own ways.[22]

A salient activity of the stallion, and maybe a boundary mark of his presence in an area, is his habit of pyramiding his dung heap. Mares do not deposit their excreta in one location again and again. The stallion's heap, which was a sign to mustangers that horses were close by, might reach a height of two or three feet. Harry Webb told me that a wild stallion's dung heap was something of a signpost which let other stallions know that an area was occupied. Harry has seen an investigating stallion smell at another stallion's heap and then lead his mares away in another direction. Once Harry caught a stallion in a rope foot trap which he placed close to the stallion's dung heap. Afterwards, and with no addition to the heap, another stallion and his mares moved into that area.

The stallion is so authoritarian that he has earned the nickname, harem master. None may leave or enter his herd without his permission, and the former is probably impossible except when a mare leaves to give birth.

Mares accustomed to herd life accept a stallion's dominance, which is probably based on fear, for a stallion can be brutal until his authority is accepted. When a stallion claims a new mare he assumes mannerisms that Will James has described as "looking wicked." The stallion closes in on the mare and drops his head until his lips virtually skim along the ground. With outstretched neck and head and ears lying flat against his skull—a warning of dire intent—the stallion races against the mare and takes bites at her. Then he may wheel and kick at her until she is driven into the herd. No mare challenges his authority for long, and mares herd immediately when the stallion goes into that motion.

iii

Spring is the feverish time for the herd. From about March to June, mares foal. Streams break through the ice and begin to run freely, and the grass is sweet and fresh—a hearty introduction to the world for a newborn foal. Most mustangers will say they have seen many colts born in deep snow, but this is exceptional. Mares come into heat most favorably for conception in the spring months. Gestation is eleven months, and birth usually occurs during the favorable conditions of the following spring. Occasionally a mare has an early heat that causes her to drop her young in the waning winter months.

A mare continues to graze with the herd until an instinctive voice tells her it is her time for giving birth. She leaves the herd for a secluded spot and might be absent for one or two days. This is one time the stallion does not interfere when a mare leaves the confines of his jurisdiction. In fact, before fencing crisscrossed the rangelands, a mare often returned to the same secluded spot on her home range year after year to give birth.

The foal is born helpless, but does not remain that way for long. Within an hour or two it has struggled and learned to stand and take milk from its dam. Within forty-eight hours, with legs practically their full size, the foal will follow its mother and take unsteady gallops. By the end of a week, two at the most, the foal will nibble grass, taste water, and frolic with other foals.

Until this moment the mare is acutely protective of her young since it has no knowledge of social order or danger. Many mares are hostile when other foals come near their young. Thus a mare exercises constant supervision over her foal, which has no fear and much curiosity. This close protection continues until the foal is capable of running from hostile gestures of other mares and other dangers. When mare and foal become separated during a chase, however, the mare rarely returns for her foal, and it will wander on its own. By contrast, a cow will return for her calf, which will stay in the area in which it became separated from its mother.

If the mare had a foal the previous season, she relinquishes her interest in the older foal in favor of the younger. Rejected and confused, the yearling persists in staying close to its dam. But her consistent and sharp attacks convince the yearling it is now a herd member and must learn a new set of social values. Some herd stallions may drive yearling colts* out of the herd, although most observers report that this occurs when the colt is about two years old and has begun to show interest in the mares. However, a few yearlings have been known to exhibit courting interest.

I have read just once, and have not had verification from any other source, that the stallion also drives yearling fillies out of the herd. This would prevent inbreeding within the herd.[23] Incest is not uncommon among domesticated horses, and inbreeding is often practiced in breeding programs to establish particular traits. Little is known about whether animals practice incest in the wild. But lately there have been some exceptions noted to the idea that the stallion drives off all other competing males, which might indicate that maybe horses do not practice incest.

Frank Robbins has run horses all his life, first in central Nevada and later on in Wyoming's Red Rock Desert. He told me he has seen a few instances where a leader stallion allowed another stallion to mingle with the herd. But this, he noted, occurred in small herds after the numbers of wild horses on the Red Rock Desert had been decimated to relatively few herds.[24]

Similarly, Norman Bearcraft, writing about Canada's few wild horses in British Columbia, said, "Contrary to popular belief each wild horse band is not held by a single stallion. Due to the extreme hardships imposed by man on these fugitives of the wild, few mares can survive, and in the Nicola District at any rate, there are three or four stallions to every mare."[25]

Of course this may have nothing at all to do with incest. Apparently, as the above two reports indicate, animal habits change when survival is in jeopardy.

In the days of their greatest number, however, the wild stal-

* "Foal" is the generic term for any young horse. A "colt" is a male foal. "Filly" designates a young female. Rangemen years ago called a young horse of either sex a colt.

lion was invariably portrayed as the sole, dictatorial leader of a herd. While he did not allow another stallion to share this role, an aged mare was often designated as second in command and was frequently observed leading the herd. This would indicate that the stallion was the *dominant leader,* an animal which may drive a herd rather than literally leading it. Since the stallion has been known to act in both capacities, the prevalent argument of earlier days as to whether a stallion leads or drives is academic. His changing role apparently depends on the situation.

When danger looms, wild horses follow escape reflexes rather than functioning rationally. A danger has only to be imagined, and herds have been known to run for miles, even when flight was inimical to their own safety. The herd itself will act in panic. But what it lacks in decision-making competence seems to be offset by the leader's abilities. The stallion is a cagey chieftain. He is capable of calculating the best exit from danger for his herd or for himself. Since horses rely on flight, it stands to reason that the stallion will place himself between the herd and the danger while directing the movement of the herd. He is not physically in the lead, but neither is a general when a maneuver is under his supervision.

Frank Lockhardt in his story of Black Kettle, a wild stallion known far beyond the borders of Kansas in the 1880s, made one of the few perceptive observations on the arrangement whereby the mare leads and the stallion drives:

> Wild horses are always led by the same mare. . . . By some signal which mystifies me, Black Kettle would turn his mares in any direction he chose without seemingly making a move. I always thought he made the signal with his ears but was never sure. He would increase or lower their speed by a slight movement of the head, which was imperceptible unless you watched him very close. The lead mare kept her eye on him at all times but the balance of the herd had no responsibility except to follow the lead

> mare, and if one of them dropped out of place even for a few steps, the male was right there to put her back.[26]

Will James was aware also of the mare and stallion relationship: "Going to water or following a trail some old mare is always ahead with the colts following. . . . The only time a stallion may take the lead is when the herd is in a pinch and crowded."[27]

This appears to be counter to the previous view of the stallion placing himself between the herd and the danger in order to direct the escape with facility. Of course, most reports say that the stallion leads. But stallions have also been known to lead for a while and then high-tail out of the country and leave the mares. One mustanger said that he had learned not to bother with a herd that the stallion was leading instead of driving because the stallion could not be trusted to keep the herd together.[28] Some wild horse runners believe this could be true. Without the stallion driving and keeping the herd intact, weaker or less disciplined horses would splinter away. And since stallions captured along with their herds have jumped corrals for their personal freedom, it may be possible that a stallion will lead for two reasons: either he is a coward stallion—and they exist—who wants to keep the herd between himself and danger, or else he is a stud who feels escape is no longer possible for the herd and is thus willing to abandon his mares in order to save himself.

What is less open to discussion is the stallion's vigilance. It is perpetual as long as he lives. At no other part of his *querencia* is it as sharply honed as at the water hole, an ancient battleground of swift death for horses. Here, predators lie and wait, so the old-time mustang and the wild horse of today approach the water hole with utmost concern. Rufus Steele has given the most satisfactory account of a herd's approach to a water hole:

> Ordinarily the approach to the spring is an almost incredible example of wariness. The family moves only un-

> der the leader's command, and he will begin to halt and sample the wind when still one or two miles away. The approach is in short advances, each followed by a standstill in which the signs are subjected to every test known to equine intelligence. . . .
>
> The fact that he has found a certain spring safe, day after day, or even the fact that another band still on the horizon has drunk its fill in peace, carries hardly a feather's weight of conviction with him. . . . He may advance and retreat many times during half an hour, or half a day, but, unless prolonged thirst had carried him to the point of desperation he must be completely satisfied or he will not come down or allow one of his mares to come to the muddy pool.[29]

The cougar was the constant nemesis of the horse. One rancher told me that a lion some years ago killed nineteen horses one mile from his ranch house in Elko County.[30] Cougars rarely pursue a herd, but have been known to do so when it includes small foals, which are the first to fall away from the herd when stampeded. The cougar has always stood a better chance lying in wait upon a rock ledge or tree limb along a wild horse trail. The horse can use his eyes to see ahead or to both sides at the same time, but cannot see up with equal ease. The cougar strikes from above onto the back of the horse. In a moment the horse is raked deeply by the hind claws while fore claws and teeth grab at the neck and throat. Unless the horse can sidestep a cougar's leap or rid itself of the cat immediately, the attack is fatal through a broken neck. Some horses have escaped and "may be identified on the range by scars they wear and nearly always the mean, terrible marks on the neck."[31]

A "killing winter" offered the worst assault. Within limits the wild horse can tolerate and adapt to extreme cold temperatures. It will paw through snow to uncover feed and does not drift in the helpless suicidal way of cattle. Horses will face a storm and huddle close to each other, or seek shelter in a canyon. Their hair grows long and thick and gives them considerable protection. Cold in itself rarely kills horses, but deep snow that makes pawing for grass almost impossible, or freezing weather of long duration which forms a hard snow crust over the land will bring on mass starvation in wild herds.

The winter of 1932, similar to the winter of 1884, killed thousands of horses in northern Nevada and southern Idaho on the Owyhee desert. Horses were seen eating at each other's manes and tails after they had chewed exposed sagebrush to its stumps. In Rattlesnake Canyon, a steep boxlike canyon off the Owyhee River, spring revealed the entire canyon floor covered with carcasses, and for years after one could only walk through the canyon over the bones of wild horses.[32]

The business of living has never been easy for the wild horse. Nevertheless, wildness imbued it with the tenacity to hold its own against predators, blizzards, and drought, and through the changing and crowding conditions in the West.

But against predacious man it was almost impossible.

With quirt hanging from his wrist and the look of pride in his bearing, "Pete" Barnum was king of the mustangers in Nevada. But when horses were no longer to be used under saddle, and were ground up for chicken-feed, he quietly departed from Nevada.

The Indians made up a small legion of tough, doughty riders, supreme in the often dangerous but sensational pursuit of wild horses. No entrepreneur who seriously wanted to make a business of rounding-up mustangs could fail to include Indians in his string of riders.

Wiry mustangs were virtual sticks of dynamite, and man was the fuse that set them off. Not all mustangs put up a scrap, but when they did, their bucking included a desperate repertoire rarely seen today.

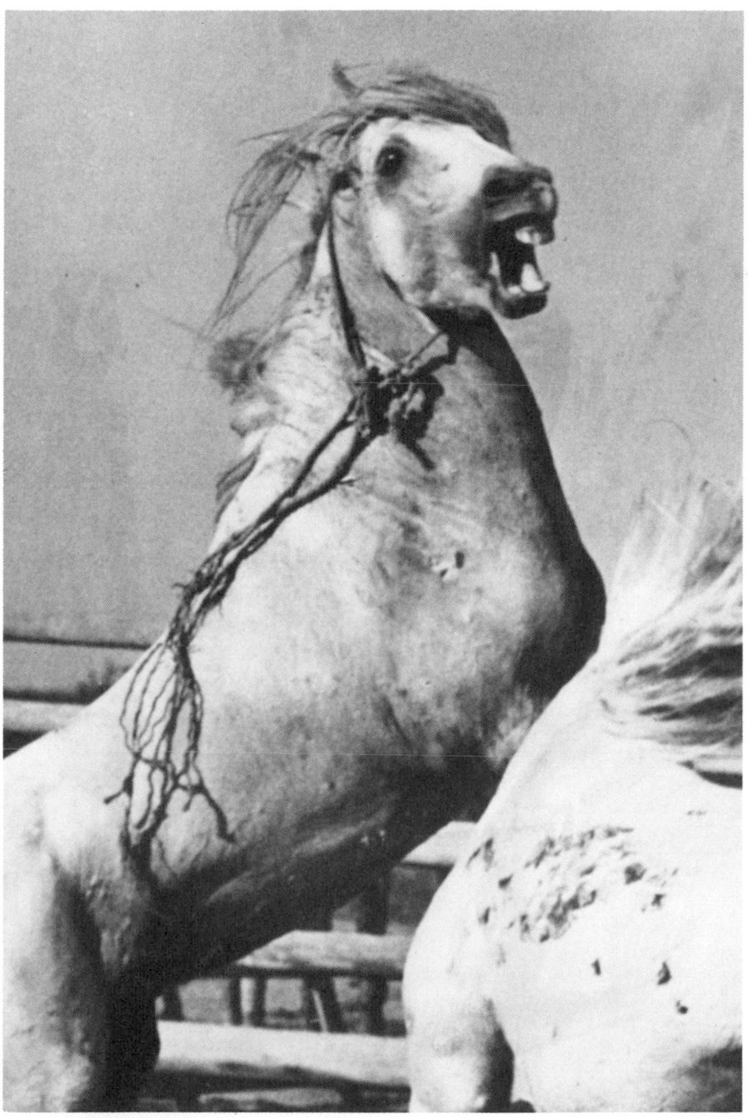

Only the greenest dude on Nevada's wild horse ranges would measure the temper of a wild horse against that of one leather-bound to man. Anyone witnessing a wild stallion fight was quickly convinced that the wild ones were to be admired through a wary eye.

"Pete Barnum's brilliantly simple canvas corral revolutionized wild horse capturing. The corrals were easily portable on mule-back, and Barnum was thus able to enter some of the last sanctuaries of the Nevada wild horse.

The bucking horse gave rodeo its fanfare and established the image of the cowboy and the wild bronc. Elko, Nevada, provided some of the toughest wild horses ever to challenge a cowboy's prowess. (Courtesy of Nevada Historical Society)

Harry E. Webb, rancher in western Nevada, mustanger supreme, and participant in the final glow of such glamorized shows as the Buffalo Bill Wild West extravaganzas. He later wrote of his horseback experiences in dozens of books and articles.

"It's uncanny," said a mustanger, "to describe the sensations that overwhelm you when chasing after mustangs. It's like you were trying to capture their freedom for yourself." But this was true only for those

men who felt depressed after they had denied freedom to some exceptional mustang. (Photo by Lew Gourley)

After passage of the Taylor Grazing Act in 1934, this scene was repeated a thousand times over. Considered to be predators of grass, wild horses were rounded up and sent to pet-food processing plants, and the former paradise for wild horses—Nevada—had seen the last of its vast herds. (Courtesy of Darrell Fullwidder)

On the Sodaville to Tonopah stage line, wild horses were frequently green-hitched for the run. Some fought violently. Some finally had to be shot because of injury. (Courtesy of Bob Robertson)

Old Whitey was a living relic. When captured in the early 1970s, running in southern Nevada with a band of wild horses, examination of his teeth indicated that he was 53 to 55 years old. A UP brand on his neck verified that he had been used as a pack mule when the Union Pacific Railroad was being laid in 1915. A few years later he was found dead on the range, killed by a bullet. (Courtesy of National Mustang Association)

One of a number of camel-looking horses captured in Churchill County, Nevada, in the late 1920s. These gave rise to the idea that wild camels had crossed with mustangs. Wild camels did indeed run wild once in Nevada, and the legend, along with the strangely shaped horses, persisted into the early 1940s.

Curly horses were another of the strange equines that ran loose in Nevada. They became the stuff of legendary story-telling among Nevada mustangers. (Photo courtesy of American Bashkir Curly Registry)

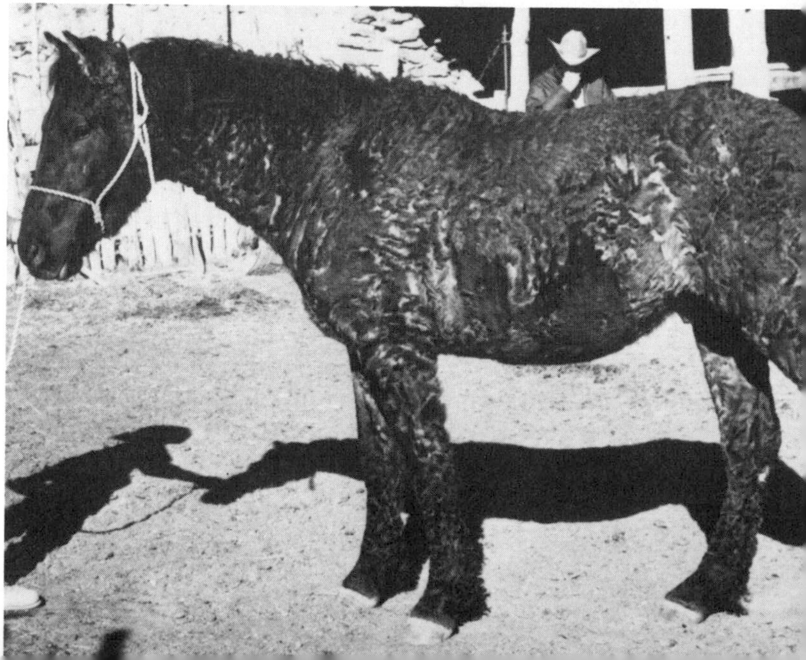

5

Tales the Mustangers Told

The wild stallion that avoided capture became a horse of legendary attributes. The longer his spirit and cunning kept him free, the more men chased him as a prize.

Often the stallion was the best horse within a herd and could sell for a higher price than the mares. If gelded, broken, and trained properly, he could develop into a good cow horse. Some were fine enough to be used as sires.

One other motive drew a mustanger's eye to the stallion: "we just wanted him anyhow because he was so much harder to catch."[1] This reason, probably more than any other, created stories of famous wild stallions.

Tales of extraordinary mustangs belong only to the horseback mustangers, not to those who would scout and pursue from a plane. The man with the engine drone in his ears rather than the heaving breath of a horse underneath him was detached from complete involvement. He was more inclined to revel in his prowess as an aerial performer than in any passion for horses. Certainly by the time planes were in vogue the horse was more a commodity for chicken feeders than for actual work use. And since horses had little chance to escape from a plane, it was rare that any single horse could distinguish itself through a clever escape maneuver.

But in the days of the horseback men, when part of a herd broke away from a mustanger's drive it was the better horses that won the reprieve. Here was a seed from which to grow a story. Doubtless, too, the old-time mustanger was a better witness to his way of life. His experiences were in depth and on more even terms with the pursued. Chasing wild horses pulled deeply from inside a man. The excitement of the pursuit, the dangers, the fifty-fifty partnership with his horse that carried him into the chase, and the passion that motivates the lover of horses all mixed together for a way of life that pulsated with clannish identity.

Here was inducement for stories of unusual and wondrous wild horses. And from campfire to campfire, as mustangers matched stories, imaginative retelling gave them added enchantment. If some of these lustrous mustangs later turned out to be rather ordinary wild horses once they were captured, what is really the difference? Better the mustangers' emotions and language fused to give their particular poetry to the land, than no recounting at all.

Some of the stories are true. Some are exaggerated. Some may even be pure fiction. But they are part of the memory of a life that can be no more.

ii

The idea that some horses preferred death to bondage smacks suspiciously of anthropomorphism. It implies conscious choice, which man claims as his own distinction. Yet some motivation causes animals to take one course over another. Emotion changes animals just as surely as emotion sometimes causes men to make unwise choices. Virtually any long-time mustanger can tell of wild horses simply dying after capture and without obvious reasons.

Some years ago a lone stud was captured. His eyes mirrored fury as he fought and charged his captors. He was finally put into a holding pasture with another captured bunch. When the men returned after a month they found the stallion dead. Neither strenuous overheating nor starvation had killed him. Feed and water were available and he was described as being fat as a seal. A cowboy claimed the horse just died of a broken heart.[2]

Others might fight on until utter exhaustion brought death. In 1913 a splendid stallion was captured in Elko County. He fought every hand that attempted to get close to him. Finally the stallion was roped and thrown. When he and his small band of mares were started toward a ranch, the stallion was "necked" to two other gentle horses. (A rope was looped about his neck and each end of the rope tied to the gentle horses on each side of him.) The stud must either follow or be dragged to death. For miles he fought, holding back. When the rope painfully wrenched his neck he spurted forward, and then held back again. His unrelenting efforts to regain his liberty ended when he fell dead between the two horses.[3]

For some years, a big lone chestnut stallion had eluded pursuers in the cedar covered mountains which divide Antelope and Monitor valleys in eastern Nevada. Traps he easily discovered. And horseback pursuers he led into the thick timber that ensured his escape.

In the winter of 1905 deep snow forced him out of his mountain retreat and into the valley. There he mingled with other herds that also had drifted down. The next spring three riders located the old renegade stallion and planned a relay chase. One rider rode a wide circuit and took after the horses for about two miles. Weaker horses dropped behind while the stallion stayed far ahead. A second rider cut in and continued to keep the stallion running. When the third rider spurred his horse from cover, he was on the heels of a fatigued stallion. Still, the pursued stayed far ahead and the vaquero began to realize that his only chance was a long throw with his rawhide riata. It was a good throw. The loop snared onto the stallion's throat, leaving only eighteen inches of riata in the rider's hand to wrap around the saddlehorn. But it was enough and the horse choked until he went down from exhaustion.

The stallion's desperation to get free never left him. He was thrown each time he attempted to run, and was continually thrown until fatigue left him prostrate. But each time a man approached with bridle and saddle he attacked with teeth and hooves so that he had to be thrown to be saddled. When he was cinched up and let loose he hurled himself over backwards crashing against the binding saddle.

He never gave up trying to find his lost life in the cedar mountains. One day his opportunity came. He made an attempt to jump a stockade corral. It was too high. He crashed on top of the heavy uprights and impaled himself. A shot from a forty-four ended his quest for freedom and his misery among men.[4]

A horse's preference for freedom in death rather than no freedom at all probably resulted from frenzy rather than true preference. Nonetheless, to witness a suicidal action brought a torturing sense of guilt to some mustangers, and a solemn respect for the horse. Two of the most famous incidents of self-destruction belong to Nevada.

Stampede was a big chestnut stallion that eluded capture for about eight years. He was reared in the Cortez Mountains in Eureka County and had remarkable surefootedness and astonishing speed. These attributes he inherited from his mustang dam and a sire believed to be a Thoroughbred that had been turned loose in the mountains to "breed-up" the mustangs for market. Stampede's qualities attracted notice from mustangers.

A number of expeditions set out after him, but he was too fleet and agile once he reached the rocky sections of the mountains bordering the valley. The easy way he slipped from pursuers and his marvelous speed had earned him his name. In earning his name he also earned a reputation. A wild horse with these two credentials became a target for every mustanger in the area, as well as some who came from afar with adventurous hopes. To catch him would be a feather in a buckaroo's hat.

One of Pete Barnum's mustangers was a young Shoshone named Nookie, a reckless rider and as wild as the horses he quested for. He, too, wanted Stampede. One summer day he hid himself and his horse behind a mass of brush-covered boulders close to a high mountain spring where Stampede led his band to water. In time Stampede approached the spring and when satisfied that no danger lurked, he drank. Nookie let him drink fully to handicap him if a chase became necessary.

Nookie threw his riata in a lightning perfect throw just as the stallion lifted its head. Stampede erupted against the riata, forcing Nookie's horse to its knees and yanking the coils from Nookie's hand. Stampede whirled and plunged up the mountain side; then turned and galloped down. Just as his legs reached their full and powerful driving speed the riata caught itself under a pine stump and twisted Stampede end for end. He struggled against the line. It tightened the choke hold on his neck until he started to gasp and his eyes bulged from the strain. It was a marvel that the riata held.

Nookie rushed the stallion with his second riata. Stampede, already in a weakened condition from his choking struggles, was easily roped and thrown. According to Barnum, when he rode onto the scene, Nookie was executing a dance of joy, for all alone he had taken the race horse stallion that had defied capture for eight years.

Stampede was not difficult to break, although two men were always required to bridle him. When worked away from other horses he obeyed reining and other commands, showing potential as a fine cow horse. When chasing wild horses however, Stampede would race to the head of a herd as if he delighted in running away with Nookie. Nookie used spade and ring bits, but to no avail. Stampede always fought for his head and took the lead in front of a bunch of stampeding horses.

Stampede's inclination when chasing other horses prompted Nookie to offer Barnum a plan to capture a band that had proved troublesome to catch. This herd was in the Cortez Valley, where Stampede was born.

The herd fed and ranged on a high tree-bald flat called Frenchy Mountain. No mustanger's horse was swift enough to rush with the herd down the sharp, precipitous mountain.

Nookie was confident that with Stampede's speed he could start the herd down the mountain side and divert them onto trails. Other mustangers would wait in concealment to rush the herd into the trap.

With the first hue of light through a still, dark dawn, the mustangers rode toward Frenchy Mountain. Nookie and Stampede had left earlier as they had a long climb to the mountain top.

By midmorning the mustangers were in place. Nookie started after the herd. Stampede immediately raced to take the lead as Nookie worked helplessly on the reins to steer the stallion.

The herd rushed toward the edge of a high-walled canyon and wormed along the edge—but Stampede did not swerve. He headed straight to the brink as Nookie jerked furiously on the reins. Stampede would not turn. His head and neck jutted straight out, his mouth set like cement against the seesaw cutting of the bit that Nookie worked with the reins.

Pete Barnum watched the episode with binoculars from a vantage point. When he observed Stampede's charging speed he knew a tragedy was about to happen. And it did. Said Barnum: "I shall always believe that the last hundred yards to the brink was covered with a burst of speed. Stampede did not tumble over the edge—he leaped. For an instant I saw a man on a horse silhouetted against blue sky. Under them, over them, around them was nothing but air." Afterward Barnum and his riders struggled with their horses around the thick brush slopes that led to the back-hanging cliff. They found the broken bodies of Nookie and Stampede amidst sagebrush and rocks. They had fallen and tumbled almost three hundred feet.[5]

A beautiful horse was no less desirable to mustangers than a beautiful woman. For nearly three years, men who knew Blue Streak gave up hearth, home and even family to chase the stallion in the mountain and valley country of southern White Pine and Eureka counties.

Most of all it was Blue Streak's color that startled the eye of the horse chasers. He was as blue-black as an eggplant, with white stockings and a prominent white blaze on his face. His conformation was magnificent. He wore his beauty in a style that excited those who viewed him in a setting as wild as he.

But Blue Streak was seen only in the winters. When heavy snows made pawing for grass difficult for him and his mares, he led his band down into the lower elevations. Mustangers around Indian Creek learned to watch for him and then give pursuit. But Blue Streak had learned that jumping was his way out of predicaments. Invariably he selected routes that posed obstacles for his pursuers. He had taught his mares to jump, too. No chase for Blue Streak could be sustained in the type of country through which he led the pursuers.

In the early decades of this century, when Blue Streak was about six years old and had appeared for the third winter in the valley near Indian Springs, twenty determined men waited to chase and encircle him before he could reach the rougher mountain slopes. But Blue Streak fooled them again. A local rancher named Rube Terrill confessed that chasing Blue Streak was getting to be "as bad as booze and poker."

One early spring Rube and two of his riders rode over to

Cockalorum Springs on the southern Eureka County line to drive out some saddle horses for roundup work.

"Are my eyes crazy?" Rube asked in a whisper.

There, in the middle of his ranch horses, stood Blue Streak. The men concluded that the stallion must have been separated from his mares, probably because of mustangers, and had wandered out of the mountains to Rube's saddle horses. Rube surveyed the fence line that held the horses in the pasture and saw no break. Blue Streak had obviously jumped the fence to join the herd.

Nearby the enclosed pasture was an eight-foot-high corral which was occasionally used as a trap when all springs but Cockalorum went dry. Rube dismounted and with a few handfuls of pebbles started driving the horses into the corral. Blue Streak herded gently along with the band, dumbfounding Rube. Even more damaging to the reputation of Blue Streak was how easily he submitted to saddle and man. It all seemed very queer for a horse that had been so wild and devious. Rube announced a conviction that when the time came—ten days or ten years—Blue Streak would make his bid to be free again.

Rube enjoyed the notice that he attracted when he rode Blue Streak into the small mining camp called Minersville. Blue Streak was at his best prancing with pent-up energy in the excitement of the surroundings.

One man hollered out an offer of five hundred dollars for the stallion. "Seven hundred wouldn't touch him," Rube responded.

A stranger in town named Abner Temple, a Salt Lake City mining tycoon and a lover of good horses, walked up to Blue Streak and put his hand on the stallion's face. "I guess a thousand dollars might take him," he suggested. Rube agreed. That afternoon a private boxcar was arranged to carry Blue Streak to Salt Lake City.

In the Mormon town, Blue Streak was a sensation every time he appeared on the streets. Abner Temple boasted that he had never felt a horse under him like Blue Streak. Within a week two attempts were made to steal the stallion. Padlocks were put on the windows and doors of the stabling area.

One night, about a month later, a tremendous commotion came from the stable, awakening Abner and others of the household. They rushed to the stable and found a section battered as if by a sledge hammer. The stallion was gone.

Abner was appalled by the brazen thieves. He offered a thousand-dollar reward and no questions asked if his prize stallion were returned. No response was elicited. Abner increased the reward.

Meanwhile, Salt Lake police carefully watched the movements of horses shipped from the city. They believed the thief to be a fool to think that a remarkable looking horse like Blue Streak could be moved without being spotted. Strangely enough, neither word nor sighting of the horse was reported. No hint at all until a farmer on the Nevada line read about the theft in a newspaper and sent word to Abner Temple that a black horse with white markings had torn a hole in his fence and then disappeared. The farmer wanted five dollars for damages.

Abner began to wonder. Now he examined more closely the sledge marks on the battered stable section. They weren't sledge marks, he concluded, but the sharp cutting edge of horseshoes. Blue Streak had made his own escape.

Abner took to his automobile and attempted to trace the stallion's westward route. At isolated farms and houses he pieced together bits of the puzzle. Blue Streak had been seen only at night. Obviously he was hiding during daylight. Also, Blue Streak was travelling on a route roughly paralleling the railroad. If Blue Streak followed his homing course along the tracks, Abner surmised, he would have to cross a small bridge near the Nevada line.

Abner Temple drove to that site. The bridge keeper reported that no horse had crossed the bridge nor had he seen one in the vicinity. Delighted with the news and sure he would retrieve his stallion in the area, Abner waited.

How long he waited no one knows. But eventually news was

brought to him that a farmer crossing a bridge over a wash about twenty-five miles upstream had had a near-serious accident when his team of horses was spooked by a "black ghost that shot past" while he was driving his team over the bridge.

Abner realized that there was now no hope of catching Blue Streak until the horse arrived back on its home range. He shipped his car back to Salt Lake City and went on to Minersville by train. From there he was taken to Indian Springs.

Abner arranged with Rube Terrill to organize a party of horsemen to search for the horse. They rode for days, and chased many bands, but never sighted Blue Streak. Then, about a week later, in a difficult region, the mustangers came upon a chewed-up piece of ground and a dead sorrel stallion. Half his bones were broken and his neck was badly lacerated. Later in the afternoon, while searching country through binoculars, Rube spotted Blue Streak. He was master of fifteen mares that had belonged to the dead sorrel.

Rube returned to the ranch and reported to Abner that Blue Streak had been located. But, added Rube, Abner would have to wait until winter when Blue Streak made his pilgrimage to the lower pastures. It was impossible to chase him now in the rugged mountains.

"You don't understand," Abner stated pointedly, "I want my horse right now."

Rube argued that five parties of mustangers would be required to get Blue Streak out of his mountain fastness, and at that it was still only a possibility.

Abner took out his checkbook and wrote a check that convinced Rube it was worth a try.

For a whole month the crews of mustangers pursued a hard-riding, fruitless course. Whenever they found a water hole they surrounded it and waited for the stallion to show. But Blue Streak sensed the presence of men and led his mares elsewhere. Nor could he be tricked into taking his familiar trails where the mustangers waited to rush him from all directions.

Finally the mustangers decided to "widow" him. Hard, strenuous riding for a few days resulted in capturing nine of his mares. Afterwards, however, Blue Streak no longer could be sighted. For a week Rube's crew searched in split groups which covered all the haunts of the wild horses. There was no trace and the men returned exhausted to Rube's ranch. That seemed to be the end of it, at least for the time being.

Then, surprisingly, news of Blue Streak came from a Paiute Indian named Roki. He had spotted the stallion and a few mares in the heart of his own mountain country about a hundred miles from Rube's ranch. Roki instructed Rube to come—"I have him in hair ropes when you get here. Better you bring much money."

Roki knew every inch of his country. It was a weird-looking assortment of mountains, benches, and hard-to-reach plateaus. Part of one mountain was shaped like a crouching lion with high granite sides. To get to the top one followed a broken trail along the lion's tail. It was also the only way down.

When Rube's mustangers arrived, Roki had not captured the stallion in his hair ropes. But Blue Streak had been pushed to the weird-shaped mountain. Now the chase began again.

Blue Streak led his mares up the trail, along the back of the lion. Blue Streak seemed to realize as the sides of the mountain dropped off into bluffs that he was being trapped. But there was no other way to go. He continued climbing, his mares behind him, and approached the rough-hewn shape of the lion's head. A jag of mountain jutted out, like an ear, for about a hundred yards. When Blue Streak reached this point he was trapped. He whirled around only to find the Paiutes spread out around the base of the ear.

Roki lowered his rope and slowly walked his horse toward Blue Streak. The other Indians watched for Blue Streak to make his break. If the stallion slipped by Roki, they were ready to rush and surround him.

Blue Streak held his head high, but his wide eyes reflected

a sense of being trapped. He surged forward. Roki responded with an upright arm ready to throw his rope. Then Blue Streak whirled, dashed through his mares and over the edge of the lion's ear. In a panic his mares rushed after him and followed Blue Streak to their death on jagged rocks below.

Rube Terrill said he would forever recall the popping explosions of the horses crashing against the earth. Blue Streak, who had been so easy to catch the first time, refused ever to be caught again.[6]

iii

In the Goose Creek Mountains that join Nevada and Idaho, a tale was told of violent conflict between father and son and the son's dispirited end. But the story is about wild horses, not people.

A proud stallion ruler of remarkable color had caused the desire for possession to glimmer in mustangers' eyes. A golden glow to his coat, neither sorrel nor buckskin but a peculiar hue, earned him the name, the Golden Stallion.

Many expeditions set out to capture the stallion, but the sight and smell of man only doubled his caution. He stayed free.

On the Old Oregon Trail, a decade or two before the close of the nineteenth century, the Golden Stallion observed an emigrant camp of wagons and horses. Instinct prompted him to add to his harem. He drove his mares to a canyon and left them to graze while he returned to watch activities at the emigrant camp.

It was not unusual in those days for emigrants to take well-bred stallions and mares with them to the new country of the west coast. In this particular herd the Golden Stallion spotted a bright bay Hambletonian mare. Her blood heritage was that of the speedy road horses of the time.

The Golden Stallion watched her from a distance. The emigrants' herd of horses was slowly grazing away from the wagons when the Golden Stallion made his move. Before the herd was aware, the stallion was in the midst of attacking the Hambletonian mare viciously. She screamed and attempted to escape, but the stallion rammed her, dropping her to her knees. He bit her to drive her from the herd; then raced alongside attacking with his teeth along her neck and shoulders until she moved in the direction he dictated.

An attempt was made by the emigrants to regain the prize mare, but they were neither equipped to sustain a chase nor had the time for a lengthy pursuit.

Riders who wanted the Golden Stallion now saw a prize catch also in the Hambletonian mare. As was typical, she became wilder than the rest of the herd and as uncatchable as the Golden Stallion.

After a year she had her foal, a colt the color of his sire. As the colt matured, his muscular and well-proportioned form showed his inheritance from his dam. Men had noticed these exceptional qualities and named the colt Silvertail.

Then, as the story goes, the inevitable struggle began. The Golden Stallion recognized the power threat in his son and ran Silvertail away from the herd, as he did all young contenders. Silvertail never stayed away for long. He periodically returned and challenged his sire, and was whipped. But one day the son defeated the old monarch. Beaten and broken, the Golden Stallion faced the fate of many aged stallions. He retreated from the herd and disappeared to live alone.

Experience in outwitting pursuers is not inheritable, and maybe Silvertail lacked the keen wisdom of his sire. For one day a group of riders accidentally came on Silvertail and his herd grazing near a water hole where an old corral was built by mustangers years before. The riders fanned out in a formation, and with pistol shots and yelling they stampeded the horses into the corral. Silvertail was caught in body, but not in spirit. When the first rope squeezed around his neck he fought with all the wildness of his nature. A number of other ropes were thrown on him—and he was pulled along to a valley ranch. The mares were released.

Living in the valley was a horseman named Billy Johnson. He wasn't a buckaroo, or even a good rider. But he was gentle with horses, slow and meticulous in handling them and winning their confidence. The mustangers put the horse in Johnson's care because all Silvertail had done so far was to fight maniacally and refuse to eat. The stallion was again roped and virtually dragged to Johnson's place.

Silvertail refused Johnson's low-keyed approach for days upon days. Finally, however, he started accepting feed from Johnson. No one but Johnson was allowed near the horse, and no voice other than his was Silvertail allowed to hear. Eventually, Silvertail submitted to saddling and allowed Johnson on his back.

Some months later, Johnson was invited to a party. A group of cowboys stopped by his place to pick him up and ride along together to the festivities. When the cowboys arrived, Billy Johnson was waiting, sitting on Silvertail. Johnson delighted in showing the horse for the first time, and along the way conversation focused on the horse's good looks and behavior.

The route took the chatting cowboys to a ditch carrying water. Silvertail approached with spooky eyes. Johnson clucked to the horse and pressed his heels to the horse's rapidly breathing sides. When Silvertail refused to leap the ditch, Johnson struck the horse with his quirt.

Like lightning, Silvertail leapt into the air and over the ditch. Before he even landed he bucked. Johnson was unprepared and as he was falling out of the saddle Silvertail struck him full force with a hoof. Then he whirled and trampled Billy Johnson to death with fearful rakes of his front hooves. The horse then disappeared into the night. It all happened in moments, leaving the cowboys stunned.

Next morning some of the cowboys followed Silvertail's trail. When they were certain that the murderous horse was heading back to his old range and his mares, they smiled to each other and turned about and rode home. They knew what would happen.

Silvertail located his mares which were now led by a young stallion. The challenger prepared to battle, but the young stud avoided any confrontation. And when Silvertail approached his mares, he was met with passive indifference.

Yes—the cowboys that had tracked Silvertail knew that Billy Johnson's way with horses had much to do with surgery. Silvertail was a gelding.[7]

iv

He was called Old Spook by an Indian mustanger named Dicey. Harry Webb, who finally caught the strikingly marked pinto, called him "everything in a mule-skinner's vocabulary" before he finally had the horse under saddle.

Dicey knew the most about the stallion that ran the ridges and coulees of the Cortez Mountains. He was out of a wild mare by a hot-blooded stallion that had escaped the Dean Ranch.

Old Spook didn't have the usual pinto markings of white and black or white and roan. He was jet black except for his white head and white stockings that went up to his knees and hocks.

The pinto had his own band when he was captured for the first time by Charley Walker and his Indian mustangers. For a pint of whiskey, Dicey was encouraged to ride the oddly-marked horse.

Dicey was flying high on the bellowing pinto when the latigo broke, crashing Dicey and his saddle against the stockade.

The pinto, still raging, was roped and busted to the ground. He was branded with Charley Walker's Bar H brand and gelded. The instant he was released, the pinto leaped up and attempted to scale the corral. He landed on the seven-foot-high fence, tottered there for a moment before tumbling over, and streaked for the hills.

This occurred in 1906 when the pinto was about five years

old. Four years passed before he was corralled again by Dicey and two other mustangers at a ranch in Pine Valley. Shelton Raine, one of the mustangers, decided to ride the pinto. It was like being on a giant-size firecracker. Shelton immediately grabbed for leather—a hold on the saddle horn—as the pinto crashed and splattered the corral gate. Shelton roused himself out of the wreckage as the pinto again made for the hills. But this time he hit a barbed wire fence. The mustangers rushed up to the horse, which was horribly twisted in the cutting wire. From his right breast to the top of his neck was a gash one could lay an arm in. Blood rushed from the wound.

Without a second thought for the possibility of the horse surviving, a mustanger named Jewell sent a .32/20 bullet into the pinto's neck just behind the ears. "Tomorrow morning," he remarked, "we'll get a team to drag away the carcass."

But the next morning the pinto horse wasn't there. In utter amazement the mustangers trailed the blotches of blood, and staggering hoof prints. They found spots where the pinto had fallen, but had risen and staggered on.

They all agreed it was impossible that the pinto could have survived the bullet, let alone his enormous loss of blood. Yet he did. His survival became a legend in the wild horse country of eastern Nevada, and Dicey referred to him thereafter as Old Spook.

When he was seen again (and no one could mistake his markings or the awful scars he wore), Old Spook was bone shaggy. His sleekness had faded and he no longer held his head and neck in that proud arch.

He joined with a gelding that ran on the range. For a while they were left in peace and companionship. But out of merriment, mustangers occasionally chased the horses until the chasing turned to earnest as Old Spook outwitted and outmaneuvered his pursuers. He avoided men at all costs, dodging and sneaking away when they came near.

Harry Webb also chased Old Spook many times. But not

even Harry's top-notch saddle horses could get close to Old Spook. When Harry did come upon the legendary horse for the last time, he was riding Old Blue, a placid horse Harry did chores from while working on the Hay Ranch in northeast Nevada.

Old Blue was a ridgeling, a half-eunuch, resulting from a poorly performed castration. He'd haze mares and get all excited, but was worthless. To top it all, Old Blue was also a ringtail: "Before a ringtail horse can be jumped out to head a critter he must first wind up his tail; then his brain seems to grasp the idea that he also has legs," was the way Harry explained his ringtail ridgeling.

At the insistence of an eastern friend of Harry's, named Al, who looked upon Harry as the personification of the western hero, Harry consented to try and find the pinto horse for him. Al had bought the horse from a soft-sell dealer who lowered his price because, he said coyly, the horse would have to be caught on the range.

Harry's protest was to no avail when he attempted to explain to Al that he had bought an uncatchable horse. As Harry told the story, it went this way:

> Here I was with Old Blue for a mount, a hunk of rat-eaten rawhide for a lariat, and I'm to jog twenty miles or so to *find* and *catch* an uncatchable mustang. Might as well try holding back the dawn, though, as to argue with Al, so to keep the peace and convince him I had at least tried I decided I'd go off somewhere and lay in the shade of a cutbank 'til evening, then come in with a big "No luck" tale.
>
> A smoky moon was sliding behind the high Cortez range to my west when a sudden desire gripped me to cross over and take a look-see down in the valley. Suddenly my gaze was riveted on a tiny speck that had topped a rise a mile across the valley. Mustangs. I started to move on. Then the huddled, drab picture changed color. Just how, was not

perceptible. Yet something had changed it from *just* mustangs. It looked like—By the powers of Mount Kelly, it was! No mistaking that blaze of white! My heart raced as I bent low over Blue's motionless neck. Then I had to laugh. Times on end I had come in close contact with this wily critter when I had a top mustang-horse between my knees instead of a mount that would be as useless as a plow mule.

The little group would mill around, pause, then come forward a few yards. It was Old Spook's method of looking things over. What puzzled me was the fact that he had taken up with any bunch. They came forward slowly, warily. A good thing they were looking into the sun. Growing bolder they began playing and scampering like kids as they galloped somewhat towards me on a trail that led to a mud spring near some dilapidated buildings.

They passed so close I could see the white splotch on his neck, a reminder of where the .32/20 slug had passed through. Old Spook was plenty pinched in the flanks yet he showed no signs of sweat. This told me that he had not found a safe water hole recently. Indians, preparing to catch mustangs, had "flagged" all the water holes around Stafford Mountain, Willow Corral and Scotch Gulch. For lack of other material they do this flagging by uprooting large sagebrush and standing them, roots up, about the water holes. Mustangs give these terrifying objects a wide berth. After a few days Mr. Injun slips out, removes the brush and is ready to rope any mustang that's fool enough to "tank up."

Oh, for a decent mount! Such a chance came but once in a lifetime and this was IT. The horses were nearing the abandoned homestead so, there being no cover between us, I might as well show myself. I recalled having seen a small sheep corral near the spring and I began laying plans. The mares, tame Morgans belonging to Ed Thomas, were on home ground now and should be easy to corral in any sort of pen.

Old Spook had me spotted instantly. He whirled, circled, came back a few jumps, then tore through the mildly interested mares as if he had to be in Texas by sundown. I moved closer. The corral was still there and the mares headed for it as if used to being there. Old Spook dashed back into the bunch and I whipped up. Never let a mustang slow up. That's when his noggin starts working. Before I realized it we were abreast of the open-end corral and on past it. I whipped and spurred and the mares turned easily, only to dodge past the opening going the other way. It was whip, cuss, and gee-haw Blue around until horses were going in every direction, with Old Spook running rings around the whole layout. And still, for some reason, Old Spook stayed with them. It was uncanny. I firmly believe it was ordained that I was to capture him. Spur, whip, shout, and turn, with the dust so thick I collided with a cow as she dashed out of the water hole. Dust so dense I wondered if Old Spook was still with us. He was! I cussed, cajoled, and pleaded. Poor Old Blue was so winded, so slow in turning that I came near jumping off and going it afoot. Then, without making sense, Old Spook streaked through the opening with the mares hot on his heels and Blue right among them. Tired as he was, this blasted ridgeling was running true to form and letting sex crowd all else out of his head. Seconds later, what with fighting Blue to keep him away from the mares, I had us fenced in.

With the loop ready to be tossed I eased ahead, and when Old Spook's eye told me I had reached the limit of sneaking I socked in the spurs and threw. But instead of the one quick jump needed to shorten the distance Blue only went "oomph" and rung his tail. Old Spook done a lot of milling around but didn't jump the fence so I dabbed another loop that bounced off his ears. If he just had horns, I told myself after a dozen throws, I'd of had him easy! There simply wasn't enough loop left of my twenty-foot rope to go over his head.

Then it happened. A loop no larger than a dinner plate went smack over his nose and up over his ears. I had him!

Just then about half the mares in the corral got their bellies over the rope and were taking Blue, Spook, and most of the corral with them. When the air cleared he was still tearing around on the end of the rope.

Now it was poor Old Blue's job to drag him home, and for the next five miles we played leapfrog with each other. If he wasn't up in the saddle with me he was heaving back and leading about as easy as a plow under a foot of sod. Well, if Blue could hold out and lug him up the mountain, we'd be hunky-dory once we got to the top. We'd have a downhill pull from there plumb to the ranch. But the steady drag was starting to cause trouble. The half hitches were cutting into Old Spook's nose, shutting off his wind. Wasn't much I could do, though, but keep going.

Blue was staggery tired as we neared the Cortez summit and it took frequent rests for him to navigate at all, and when I'd urge him on, his tail would go round like a windmill. I'd been guarding against this but it happened! His tail got over the rope and was clamped down on it. Now if there's one thing that will rejuvenate a fagged-out cayuse this is it. Like an explosion, Blue's nose went between his hind legs, and with Old Spook snorting and kicking we took back down the mountain in twenty-foot leaps. Between the bucking and the rope sawing into my thigh, I could neither stay on nor get off, but the problem solved itself. We all got tangled up and went rolling over and over.

The next thing I knew, the rope was parted at the saddle fork and Old Spook, now spooked aplenty, was tearing down the mountain. At sight of this my heart sank so low I never even thought of giving chase. Wasn't any use. He was a goner this time! But it just goes to show you what luck can do. No sooner had he hit the flat when he went end over end and began cutting all sorts of didoes. Hopping on one good leg to where Blue had quit rolling, I crawled on and wasn't long in getting to where Old Spook was turning back flipflops. It was plain he'd be strangled in the next few seconds for the loops around his nose had finished cutting off his breathing.

Perhaps it was sheer imagination, but I could have sworn when I loosened the rope there was a light of gratitude in his puffed, bloodshot eyes as air and life rushed back into him and he just lay there, legs twitching, sides heaving. It was then I noticed Blue had near been scalped in his roll down the mountain and, even though he had done everything wrong and wasn't worth the lead it would take to kill him, I hurriedly anchored the riata once again around the pommel, then put my arms around Blue's neck and hugged it to my throbbing face. There's something about a horse that makes a feller do those things.

Travel was slow on the homeward journey. But I can say this for Old Spook, he never once let the lead rope so much as tighten.

A bright, midnight moon found us back at the ranch, the corral gate wide open as if there was no doubt that I'd bring home the bacon. Well, I'd sure delivered the goods and expected an effusion of praise and back slapping. None came. Only: "God what a beauty!" Al kept repeating this as if reciting a litany. Finally: "Have any trouble getting him, Harry?" My mind was murdering him but I mumbled a nonchalant "Not a bit; easy as pie."

"I knew you wouldn't," he agreed. "Now tomorrow I'll break him gentle and ship him home when I go."

Al never had a chance to break Old Spook. The horse was ready to fight him and the tip of the reins was as close as Al could get. Oddly, the horse allowed Harry to approach, pet, and handle him.

Four times Harry eared the horse down while Al mounted. Four times Old Spook threw Al. The last time Old Spook threw and literally wrapped Al around the snubbing post. Al relinquished the horse to Harry and took his loss of one hundred dollars and a lot of skin.

Harry continued to work the horse in a casual, slow-paced

fashion. That seemed to be what Old Spook responded to. A few years were required until Old Spook was reliable enough to be ridden by Harry in routine cow work. For many more years afterwards, Harry used Old Spook as a mustanging horse when he was rounding up wild ones for the government.

Curiously, Old Spook never lost his fear and suspicion of an upturned sagebrush. "Mere sight of one," said Harry, "and he'd swap directions like a rubber ball thrown against a rock wall."

Old Spook lived to an old age, dying in 1938.[8]

V

Even the bizarre finds its way into wild horse lore. The colonial diary of James Kenny said that strange Indians from beyond the Mississippi told of many large horses in their country which never lie down to sleep but lean against a tree for that purpose.[9] And as recently as 1948 visitors to the Nevada State Fair saw a live camel-like horse. He was caught by several cowboys chasing after wild horses near Tonopah, Nevada.

The strange creature did not look entirely like a camel, and neither did he have all the characteristics of a horse. A hump rose from his shoulders and, like a camel and unlike a horse, he kneeled in order to eat. His gait resembled the shuffling gait of the camel, and a sloped rump backed off his hindquarters to a camel type of ratty tail.

The cowboys reported that he was an outcast living on the periphery of the herd. He would be chased away by a stallion if he tried to mingle with the mustangs.

A year later another humpbacked horse was caught, a mare, in the same vicinity where the stallion was captured. Then someone remembered that a camel-horse was trapped in 1928 in the desert north of Tonopah. All of them were considered genetic freaks until it was recalled that camels had run wild on the Nevada desert about eighty years before.

While Jefferson Davis was Secretary of War, he granted permission to a commission to import camels from the Near

East. It was anticipated that the dromedary would serve transportation needs more efficiently than horses and mules on the Great American Desert.

From 1856 to 1860 the experiment proved camels to be adaptable and efficient on the southwest desert. But Americans who had to work and ride the camels despised them. Their peculiar rolling gait brought on a nauseous desert "seasickness." And cattle and horses bolted in terror at sight of the camels. Their singular smell caused silly behavior in livestock, even before the camels appeared in sight.

When the government abandoned the camel project the animals were sold at auction. A few appeared in Virginia City soon after. Hostility manifested itself in the mining city after horse teams were frightened by the camels and went galloping wildly down the main street. The Nevada Legislature passed a law in 1875 prohibiting camels on public highways. At this time the camels were used for hauling salt from the Esmeralda Marshes southeast of Walker Lake and across the dry desert to the Virginia City mills. The camel train was required to enter Virginia City after midnight over an unused trail. During the day, because of the disturbances the camels created, they were securely locked in barns.

When salt was discovered closer to Virginia City, mules were immediately substituted for the camels which were taken out to the desert and turned loose; "Good riddance," said citizens of Virginia City.

Unmolested for some years, the number of camels increased and they were frequently seen in the central and northwestern parts of Nevada. And if chasing mustangs became a bit boring for cowboys there was always a camel to chase. One in particular, named Old Brigham, who commanded a herd of about forty camels, came under the scrutiny of some cowboys who lovingly eyed the four-foot mane. It would weave into an unusual hair rope.

One day a once-in-a-while cowboy named Joggles Wright

and a friend decided to have Old Brigham's mane. They rode to the Carson Sink where Old Brigham and his band fed.

Joggles was on a fast horse and he rode into the herd first. His lariat whirred through the air and caught the camel at its throat. As soon as Old Brigham felt the noose he laid his ears back, hissed, spit, and charged Joggles at a rapid pace. Joggles spurred his horse into a retreat. But the infuriated camel closed the gap, and the rope, which was tied hard and fast to Joggles's saddle, slackened menacingly on his horse's rear legs. Quick turning, Joggles knew, would be too dangerous with the rope leaping along. But when he started to smell the malodorous breath of Old Brigham, he knew the camel was too close. Joggles fished for his knife while reining his horse into a serpentine pattern to throw the camel off. Finally he cut the rope and sped away as fast as his saddle horse could run. He lost his rope but felt it was a cheap price to pay. Afterwards when Joggles told his story, Old Brigham was left alone by other cowboys.

Camels roamed the Nevada desert until about 1890 when they were all slaughtered. As one can imagine, tales of ghostly camels silhouetted on a desert ridge against a full moon were told until very recently. Virginia City commemorates the camel and its Comstock days with a yearly camel race event.[10]

Whether the camel-horses were a cross between camels and horses was debated for some years. As camel numbers diminished in the late 1880s some of them might possibly have joined a wild horse herd. This has been considered unlikely as horses supposedly avoided the smell and sight of the camels. But camels and horses live in close proximity in the Near East, and this, say the advocates of the hybrid theory, is what eventually happened in Nevada. Whether they would mate, however, is seriously doubted. Nonetheless, those who saw the camel-horses feel they looked too much like a camel to be just mere freaks, but were indeed throwbacks to camel-horse matings.[11]

Long before camel-horses were publicly noted another freakish horse roamed parts of Nevada's wild horse ranges.

Some mustangers called them buffalo horses (but not because they were possible offspring of a horse and buffalo union). Other appellations were fur-covered horses and curly horses. Cowboy humor could not pass them by, and described them as horses with a permanent wave. Their marcelled coat was a thick mat of tightly woven hair.

An old time mustanger named Morton Bell sketched his first encounter with them this way:

> In 1910, '11, and '12 I had a bunch of Paiute Indians helping my partner and me corral wild horses in central Nevada. I think it was in 1912 we ran into a bunch of "curly sorrels" about a hundred miles east of Tonopah. It certainly was a nice bunch of wild ones, every one sorrel and every one "curly." These horses all had tight curls. . . .
>
> Had it not been for my partner, Ed Hand, the stallion would probably have killed me. The Indians, six of them were along that day, seemed afraid of this particular bunch of curly sorrels. In the middle of our "run" I noticed that my partner and I were the only ones left in the race. The stallion wasn't more than half a mile into a blind canyon we had picked out when he sensed something wrong. He whirled and ran back behind his bunch, just as he had been doing to haze them along, only this time he kept coming straight at me. I already had my rope down, but was almost afraid to use it. . . . Anyhow I threw for his front legs when he reared up almost over me and my horse, and my loop settled over his head just as pretty as if I had really wanted it to go there. . . . Good old Ed showed up and made a neat cast on one hind leg. I got down and started to fit a quick hackamore over Curly's head so we could get him into camp (some eighteen miles). . . .
>
> I guess in trying to loosen my rope to stop from choking him, I lifted my weight off his head for a split second, and he reversed his nose and had a bulldog grip on my left leg about halfway down from my knee. I never suffered such agony before or since. I had on heavy boots and chaps and he made a pulp out of my leg in about three seconds flat. I

> didn't want to kill him as he was not only a prize catch for us, but a curiosity as well with all those tight-rolled curls. I had a big, heavy six-shooter and I prized and twisted the barrel between his jaws and all he'd do was go a little deeper. Ed yelled he'd shoot him himself, but he was so excited he was afraid he'd hit me instead. Finally, I reluctantly stuck the muzzle between his ears and pulled the trigger. . . . I was on a cane and crutches for about a month, and when I tried to round up my Paiute boys again, they all said no more riding after curly sorrels.[12]

Morton Bell wasn't the first person to see the curly horses, and any time they were seen they aroused a sense of wonderment and speculation. The Damele Ranch near Austin in central Nevada went through three generations of family ownership, and some of the curly horses were bred there from 1898 on, when the ranch founder roped three from a wild herd near the Roberts Mountains in Eureka County.

The silky, poodle-like coat is a fixed trait in these horses and allows them to withstand a cold that kills other horses. During the winter of 1932, when thousands of horses and cattle died on western ranges, the curly horses survived in their home range while virtually all other horses in the area perished. This fact was reported by Pete Damele, who also noted that the mares are heavy milkers producing four to six gallons a day.

The only known breed that matches the properties of the curly horses is bred in the state of Bashkir on the east slope of the Ural Mountains in Russia. Regions around the Black Sea and in northern China also breed this type. Albert Laird remembers when the curly horse was first brought to the United States and to Nevada.

Laird, as a boy, worked and broke horses for Tom Dixon in Eureka County, who was one of the largest breeders of horses in the state. Frequently he made trips to European countries to buy horses for his extensive breeding programs. He went to Ireland and shipped some Irish horses to Eureka, which were later followed by shipments of Clydesdales, Percherons, Shires, and Morgans from the East Coast.

Several years later, says Laird, Dixon went to India where he heard there were horses that could withstand cold temperatures and high altitudes.

> The horses were called Bashkirs, or wooly ones. He bought two mares and one stallion and brought them back with him. Both mares were in foal. After Tom had them safe in Eureka, two stallion colts were born.
>
> When the two stud colts were old enough to be turned out on the range, he took one into the Buckskin area and turned it loose with the mustangs in the valley there. The other he turned loose in Long Valley, White Pine County. It was not very long until curly horses were showing up around the valleys in the Buckskin Mine area, in Pete Hanson Canyon and that area; also Long Valley, Newark Valley, Fish Creek Valley, and Six Mile.[13]

No Bashkirs have been seen in a wild state for a decade or so. Apparently those remaining are bred at the Pete Damele Ranch. In past years, some found their way into Wyoming and Canada, and possibly some Bashkirs are now located in those areas.

What may be the last wild equus to distinguish itself belongs to the mule family and not the horse. Old Whitey, a small white mule, was until recently the oldest member of the equine family, wild or tame, in Nevada.

For many years he was seen with a small, wild band of horses in the southern Nevada desert near Caliente. Citizens there claimed he was once a pack mule that hauled supplies to road gangs laying track on the Union Pacific Railroad. A man named Frank Wilson, now dead, is said to have last worked the mule in 1915. That would have made the UP mule, as he was also called, over fifty years old.

"A mule has to be awful ornery to live that long," suggested a mustanger. So a few mustangers decided to see just how old Whitey really was.

Tom Holland, whose mustang fever runs high, but who is just as devoted to preservation of the remaining wild horses, organized a crew of men to catch Old Whitey. A plane was used to spot the herd Whitey was known to stay with. Their location was relayed to mounted horsemen who took up the chase. Whitey was easy to locate in the herd but in the weather-hewn broken country the herd frequently disappeared for moments before they were again spotted. After one such happening, Old Whitey wasn't seen with the herd. Later, when the pursuit had been abandoned for awhile, Old Whitey reappeared with his herd. The chase was renewed and again Old Whitey repeated his slick vanishing act.

Immediately it became evident to the mustangers that Old Whitey went into hiding any time the herd was chased. Ivan Hunt of Utah decided he would keep his eye strictly on Old Whitey when the chase started again. Hunt saw that Old Whitey turned back from the herd once they rushed down a brush-choked wash. There Old Whitey waited in hiding. Hunt doubled back and without any trouble cast a loop over Old Whitey's neck. Once the mule felt the old symbol of bondage he immediately tamed down.

No brand was visibly located on Whitey's hide, but a finger tip touch was able to trace the brand scar, *UP,* on his neck. If that weren't evidence enough, an inspection of Whitey's teeth, extremely slanted and worn, indicated advanced age. There was no doubt among the horsemen that Old Whitey was over a half century old. His longevity was attributed to his years of freedom and no chance to overeat, particularly in that section of the desert. This verification occurred in 1967.

Whitey was turned loose to join his band and was periodically checked by the mustangers. In 1968, two inspections noted Whitey missing from the herd. A plane flew over the area and spotted a white animal lying dead. Horsemen later rode to the location and found Old Whitey. But it was a bullet that had ended his life.

"I don't understand it," said one of the men. "He lived in peace all these years and was known just to the folks in Caliente who sort of watched over him. Just as soon as a bit of publicity came his way this is what happened. Who could do a thing like that?"[14]

6

Bronco!

In 1878, so a story goes, a "true born Englishman" named Tom came to Nevada to break wild horses for a livelihood. He was told in the understated prose of buckaroos that the sort of horses here were different from those he was familiar with.

> "Mon, a 'oss is a 'oss the world hover," Tom replied, "hand h'I've ridden 'osses after 'ounds and broke many a bad 'un. Besides, 'mon, these little fellers aren't big enough to 'ave much strength."
>
> Tom pestered until he was given a wild horse to break. The buckeroos blindfolded his bronc and helped Tom put on his "pancake saddle and snaffle bit" and held the "baste" until Tom mounted.
>
> The blindfold was whipped off and the horse stood stiff-

> legged. Tom clucked with his tongue. Then he urged with his legs. Four lightning jumps and a whirl and Tom was sailing.
>
> When he came to he described the sudden event to the buckeroos:
>
> "Why the dom baste was nothing like a 'oss. First 'e stood on 'is 'eels, and then 'e stood on 'is 'ead. Then he 'umpted 'is back like 'e was sick at the stomach and wanted to puke a bit, and then 'e came down with one of those dirty shakes, 'umpted 'is back again and hoff I went."[1]

Mark Twain met the same sort with a horse he called a Genuine Mexican Plug, shortly after he arrived in Carson City. At an auction he purchased a horse for twenty-seven dollars, saddle and bridle included. Here's how he described his first ride:

> In the afternoon I brought the creature into the plaza, and mounted him. As soon as they let go, he placed all his feet in a bunch together, lowered his back, and then suddenly arched it upward, and shot me straight into the air a matter of three or four feet! I came as straight down again, lit in the saddle, went instantly up again, came down almost on the high pommel, shot up again, and came down on the horse's neck—all in the space of three or four seconds. Then he rose and stood almost straight up on his hind feet, and I, clasping his lean neck desperately, slid back into the saddle, and held on. He came down, and immediately hoisted his heels into the air, delivering a vicious kick at the sky, and stood on his forefeet. And then down he came once more, and began the original exercise of shooting me straight up again.
>
> The third time I went up I heard a stranger say: "Oh, *don't* he buck, though."[2]

After Mark Twain and the bronc parted he reflected on the poverty of the human machinery since two hands were not sufficient to soothe all the hurt on his body.

He should have hired one of those itinerants who made their livelihood riding wild horses. A man needed skill and daring, a virtuosity that gave royal rank to those who survived the twisting, contorting antics of a wild horse.

Nothing has disappeared from the American West with more certainty than those riders, just as surely as clipper-ship sailors became only a memory when sea vessels were no longer driven by wind and sail.

Even a vocabulary peculiar to the wild horse man's profession has disappeared from Western jargon. Only those who were part of the times know the verbal currents of the bronc man. Bronc rider is still a popular term. But bronc fighter, bronc stomper—nowaways all used interchangeably—were once interpretative shades of a man's ability and style on a wild bucking horse.

Ramon Adams, who has collected and classified western words and expressions, gathered some of a bronc man's palaver:

> When the horse "hid his head an' kicked the lid off," or "warped his backbone an' hallelujahed all over the lot," the comments upon his ability were such as "he's a beast with a bellyful of bedsprings," "frolicsome little beast," "real hunk of death," "cutey, little grave-digger," "he's tryin' to chin the moon," and perhaps the rider was warned that the horse would "buck his whiskers off," or "he'll throw y'u so high the birds'll build nests in yo' hair 'fore you light," or "he'll stomp y'u in the ground so deep y'll take roots and sprout."[3]

This range lexicon of not too long ago—when riders were distinctive products of their environment, and a southwestern rider who stood apart in manner and dress from a northwestern buckaroo was not lumped with him into a literary genre called "cowboys"—displayed an array of terms specifying bucking techniques of the old-time wild horse: gut twister, pile driver, spinner, sunfisher, cloud hunter, blind bucker, and a good dozen more such terms were used to describe the tricky wild horses that no longer exist today. These particular bucking styles will be described later.

It was these "fearful and wonderful stunts" of the old-time horse that made riders, now stiff in limbs and years but whose memories quicken at mention of the historic bronc, extol them with the comment that horses today don't buck like they used to.

Bob Robertson, who was the most enlightened mind I knew on the procession of men and horses through history, told me, "I haven't seen a bucking horse in over forty years. What you see in rodeos today are not the same type of horse. They're kickers, not buckers."[4]

Neither facetiousness nor partisanship to a way of life with which he is more sympathetically identified causes that observation. Wild horses don't buck like they used to: twisting and snapping with more convulsions in a ten foot diameter than a modern rodeo horse could conceive in an entire arena. I'm not disparaging the current rodeo horses. They are bigger and stronger than their wild range predecessors and can give a cowboy a jolting time in an arena. But their genetic makeup has changed, giving them a different style of performance under saddle.

The bogged head, humped back, stiff legs, and bunched feet of the wild horses fifty-odd years ago are what gave the bronc man his profession. Some call it bucking, others call it pitching. Usage depends on where in the West one's verbal habits were formed. In those parts of the West where a cowman faces blizzards and temperatures below zero they say bucking. Where the landscape is arid pitching is the term.

Either way, the wild bucking talent was peculiar to horses in the Western Hemisphere. There is no definite theory as to the origin of this habit in American horses. One northwestern buckaroo's quip that bucking started from the back door of hell on a hot day and came out on the run might be as good as any other explanation.

Another theory suggests that bucking evolved from defensive kicking by wild horses against attacking wolves. However, this overlooks the fact that European and Asiatic wild horses were also plagued by wolf packs, yet few of those horses have been known to buck with the American bronc's vehemence.

Another idea is that American wild horses learned their style of bucking from pitching panthers off their backs. A panther, cougar, or mountain lion would drop onto the back of a horse from a tree or rock, grab for the neck with claws, and in a fluid, blurring motion, clamp its jaws underneath the horse's chin and jerk the neck upward. The twist often broke the neck of the horse. The only way a horse could possibly free itself from the cat was to duck its head deep between its legs and buck for all it was worth.

Horses that succeeded in ridding themselves of a cat by bucking presumably passed the trait on to their offspring. But as any student of biology knows, acquired characteristics are not inheritable. However, as wise Frank Dobie observed, "If an animal never acquired anything new, how would evolution ever proceed?"

Bob Robertson, I think, comes closest to an explanation of why horses buck only in the Western Hemisphere. He credits the habit to a latent instinct in hot-blooded horses—the blood of the Barb, the Arab, and other North African stock.

When their ancestors were running wild in Arabia and Asia Minor some thousands of years ago, they may have learned to counter feline attacks by humping their backs and ducking their heads between their legs to protect the jugular and the critical atlas joint between the head and the first joint on the spinal column. Zebras and wild donkeys that still live under the menace of wild cats buck in the manner of the horse.

The counter argument that bucking in Arab and African horses has not been observed must be considered in view of the horse's long history of domestication in that region. The horse was reclaimed early in man's history in that part of the world and has since never been far from the domesticating hand of the Bedouin and other mounted tribes. The instinctive need for horses to buck subsided centuries ago.

Horses of northern Europe and the Asiatic Steppes, the cold-bloods, defended themselves from their prime enemy, the wolf packs, by kicking, striking, and biting. Wolves do not attack by pouncing upon a horse, but attempt to tear at the underbelly or sever the hamstring on a horse's hind leg to render it immobile.

Thus horses defended themselves in a fashion that best met the distinctive threats. This is not to say that the cold-bloods and wild horses today cannot buck; they do, but not with the adroitness of the Spanish horses that went wild in the Americas and became the mustangs. Big cats were also prevalent in the Americas, and the horse's instinctive reaction to cat attacks brought the horse's bucking repertoire into bloom again. The "bag of bucking tricks" which became part of American wild horses is probably an ancient instinct, but it is a recent phenomenon in the Americas.

When this same blood was diluted by mingling with the many cold-blooded breeds that accompanied the advancing frontier, the temperament of the mustang changed. The mixture of the blood may have resulted in the gradual loss of ability in the wild horse to hump its back and practically touch its tail with its nose. Soon after the Taylor Grazing Act of 1934 when the government removed thousands of unbranded horses from the public range, just about all remnants of the Spanish-mustang blood disappeared. In its place, as herds again increased through strays and horses lost on the range, cold blood predominated.

In any case, early day range horses until about 1920 were typified by the bronco, the true bucker. Horses running wild during the last fifty-odd years reflect the trend to cold blood, the kickers. These now come out of the rodeo chutes with head up, back hollowed, and hind legs kicking for the moon. True, the bucking strap tightly cinched against a horse's flank does prevent actual bucking and forces a horse to kick. But without it the horse would probably dart out of the chute as a runaway, because bucking is not a strong instinct or ability with cold-bloods.

ii

Man himself, in the person of the old-time bronc rider, is probably just as much a cause of bucking as the big cats. In many ways the men were broncos themselves—raspy, rough, untamed, and whose "cowboy gentility," if any, was reserved for women and never horses. When a buster armed with spurs and quirt swung onto the back of a bronc, the horse went into a frenzy no less than if a lion had landed on its back. Bellowing and bucking, humping its back to rid itself of the dreadfulness of a man determined by pride to ride the bronc to a finish, they made a picture that embossed the American West on the world's imagination.

The heyday of the bronc rider was that time when horses were central to ranch life, and a rancher might own fifty or five hundred horses for use by hired riders. These ran wild until gathered. Larger outfits might keep one or two bronc busters on a permanent payroll to "green-break" the waspy range horses for the remuda or cavvy (the pool of ranch saddle horses).

Miller and Lux, the cattle empire that extended through California, Nevada, and Oregon, had a cavvy of about 140 horses at one of their Nevada stations called Black Rock. An equal number of horses ran wild on the range as eventual replacements. Of the fourteen vaqueros that worked at that division, three were rough string riders, or bronc riders.[5]

Smaller outfits might hire a bronc man who also rode in routine ranch and cow work. Just as frequently an itinerant bronc man rode circuit through the cow country, from ranch to ranch, breaking the "snuffy" horses.

Wages were usually a few dollars per head, sometimes five dollars if a man had a good reputation. Other deals between ranch owner and bronc rider were also popular. The bronc man might contract for a base payment for so many head to be green broke, or set a price on so much per saddle. This meant that each time the horse was saddled and ridden, usually two or three times, the rider collected a few dollars.

After the rides the horse was turned into the remuda as green-broke, but not trained. Eventually the horses were assigned to individual cowboys as part of their string of saddle horses. The cowboys were then responsible for converting them into useful cow horses.

Riding wild horses for the first time was a hazardous business. Unlike today where horses are broken and trained as two or three year olds—literally still babies—the range horse frequently ran wild until he was five or six years old, fully developed, powerful, and set in his ways. Only a young man could stand the rigors of riding bucking horses for a living, and he was old for the challenge by the time he was thirty. By then, the contest with hundreds of horses had left the marks of his profession upon him in a broken collar bone, leg, foot, or arm. Others claimed never to have suffered a broken bone—a sign, at least, that they could fall from a horse with adroitness. Virtually all bronco busters, however, lived their lives with stiffness in their joints from the bone bruising, pounding, and twisting stunts of the bucking horses. Sometimes after a man's career had ended, he became spooky about a horse bucking beneath him and would ride only the gentlest horses on a ranch.

Not all bronc men could handle the "fearful and wonderful stunts" of the bronc. Range jargon classified individual bronc men's abilities. Some men were not good horse breakers. They could take the first fighting edge off a green horse but usually in a way that still left much fight in him. So, a "bronc stomper" was a "man with a heavy seat and a light head."[6] "Bronc fighter" was a term of derision, pointing to one who did not control his own temper and would likely spoil a horse or make it into an outlaw. Bronc fighters rode wide circuits in an effort to stay ahead of their reputations.

"Bronc buster," "bronc peeler," and "bronc twister" indicated men who took pride in their work. No ranch wanted spoiled horses. Although a bronc might kick, squeal, wiggle, paw the air, pound the earth, or roar like a buffalo, as some observers described it, a rider who took the fight out of a horse and left the spirit intact for a cowboy to develop was a professional of high esteem. Such an accolade was hard to earn from ranchers and cowboys who never were casual in weighing judgments or giving praise.

Spring and summer were the bronc man's seasons. Horses in the wild were run in from their winter haunts and the herds separated into groups. Mares and spring foals were cut from the main herd, in order to brand and castrate the new colts. They were roped and thrown, branded and gelded—an upsetting experience that the young horses never forgot. When as stout five and six year olds they were again corralled, this time for breaking by the bronc man, they stared wild-eyed and frightened as they again faced a man with a rope. This time they were ready to fight.

Joe De Young, who knew range life at the turn of the century, told me: "When you speak of the tools a bronc man uses, you take guts for granted."

Beyond this, the bronc men's techniques varied as much as the style of tools they used. Some might have an assistant, usually an apprentice kid, starry-eyed and hoping to be a mighty bronc buster. Others preferred the lone wolf approach and wanted no one else around when they were working horses. Either way, a bronc man relied on artistry with a rope to throw the horse. That skill determined how well the bronc man offset a horse's strength. A quick subduing impressed the horse. Sloppy rope work that allowed the horse to fight excessively because of the rope strangling him or chafing and burning his legs caused fights of desperation. He would fight even more the next time.

Joe told me about a bronc man's rope this way: "The professional horse breaker is apt to be a very prideful, touchy sort of specimen where the details of his rig are concerned; but of all the articles, the one that receives the most careful handling is his rope. He may be careless with everything else on earth, including cash money and the spoken word, but he doesn't want anybody taking liberties with his pet rope."[7]

Probably no roper was, or still is, more particular on this point than the buckaroo west of the Rockies, as he generally used a riata. This braided rawhide is tricky to use even in the hands of one born to use it. A riata man did not need to be told if another person had been fooling with his coils because it was sure to snarl and kink in a telltale way. It was as personal in a pair of hands as the bench-made boots on the bronc man's feet. He kept his riata tallowed to keep it dry, because a damp one was apt to pull apart.

California vaqueros were the masters of the riata tradition. Most Nevada buckaroos followed the ways of the Californians with riatas, along with California spurs, saddles, and boots. Some Nevadans did prefer the east of the Rockies style—the Texas way—and used the shorter grass ropes, whale line, or maguey, and other types of Texas equipment.

When a big, raw horse was cut from the herd for breaking he was run into a small corral. He knew something was in the wind. His eyes glistened and every nerve in his body set him on anxious alert.

The bronc man entered the corral carrying his riata. The bronc usually rushed to a part of the corral farthest from the breaker. A horse might start running along the edge of the corral, which was what the bronc man wanted. By a clever, snakelike throw of the riata, the loop caught the horse on the front legs and tumbled him in a somersault to the ground. Working the riata in this critical moment required an exact feel when the horse's weight had taken enough pull to trip him. At that precise moment the breaker released part of the pressure on the riata or it would snap in two. A grass rope did not need this concern, and with it the bronc buster merely sat back on his heels, the rope worked under his buttocks, and held till the horse tumbled.

The bronc buster rushed up to the fallen, wind-busted bronc and with rapid, deft movements of the riata, hog-tied the horse's legs together. Some breakers bound the horse firmly because they believed that complete subjection forced the horse to give up more rapidly when he realized he could not fight the rope. Other bronc men wanted the horse to struggle and fight the rope and to learn that fighting only brought pain. The horse was then left to mull in his mind the recent turn of events in his life.

Usually a hackamore was placed on the horse's head soon after it had been thrown. This halter rigging, although it is not a halter, is still used today, but few are capable of drawing out its potential as did the California horsemen. In their deft and patient hands the horse worked in a hackamore up to four years before a bit would be introduced into its mouth. The hackamore, and the spade bit afterwards, was part of the California system of training that produced the finest light-reined cowhorses ever known.

Not all bronc men followed this system. A trainer named George Manning took another approach to breaking horses when he worked on the Double Square Ranch out of Winnemucca during the first decade of this century. Ed Hanks was working on the ranch at the time and told of Manning's technique this way:

> There was a big high board corral, where he'd take the horses that were to be broken, one at a time. When he got in there with his horse, he had a long whip with a lash on the end, and it would pop and make a big noise. It never hurt the horse much. He had a whipstock with a whip in one hand and a whipstock without a whip in the other hand. He would stand in the center of the corral with a wild horse running around to climb the sides to get out. He'd whip them with the whip, and it would pop like a gun. Pretty soon the horse would stop running and look at him. I never could see why they stopped but they did. Then he'd watch the horse and keep its attention on him,

sort of seemed to hypnotize them. He'd keep a steady eye and a steady hand and walk toward the horse, then he'd back away. He kept doing this, but he was getting a little closer each time, and he was keeping the horse's attention all the time. Pretty soon he got close enough to touch the side of the horse's head with the empty whipstock. Then he'd rub the horse on the side of the head, on each side with the whip and the whipstock, and finally with his hands. He used to rub his hands from near the horse's eyes, down toward his nose.

After doing this for some time, he would back away and get a halter, watching the horse and keeping his attention all the time. He had steady nerves, and he would ease the halter onto the horse gently. The halter had a long rope and he would lead the horse to the gate and give him to us. Then he was ready for another horse.

Ed said that sometimes George Manning would get a man-eater horse that would charge him. With sensible discretion, George yelled for a gate tender to let him out—quick. George would then work the horse from the gate until he "dociled" the horse and could enter the corral.[8]

Some bronco busters topping a horse for its maiden ride expected and encouraged a fight. The first time the horse was saddled little regard was given to the horse's fear. An assistant covered the horse's eyes with a rag blind and then grabbed hold of its ears, gave a twist and held on while the bronc man tossed the saddle on and tightened it to the horse's belly. Then the rider stepped into the stirrup, swung deep into the saddle and with a nod of his head the assistant tore away the blind.

But not all breakers commenced with such speed, and the bronc man's approach often depended on whose horses he was working. The mustanger who dealt with capturing wild horses and shipping them to markets usually wanted the horses green-broke quickly. The owners of horses that carried a ranch brand usually cautioned the buster to take it easy so as not to encourage any more bucking and fighting than was necessary. Nuisance buckers were detested in ranch remudas.

After a bronc had been thrown and a hackamore fitted, a slower-paced method commenced. It involved tying up one front leg by taking a couple of hitches with a soft cotton rope around the fetlock, lifting the leg until it doubled against the forearm, and then tying the end of the rope around the horse's neck. With the horse immobilized and tethered to the snubbing post in the middle of the corral, the bronc man casually worked about the horse. He might take out his pocketknife and cut the mouse nests (balled hair) out of the main and tail. All the while he made small talk to create a calming atmosphere. Next, a yellow slicker, or leg chaps, or a saddle blanket was waved and snapped in front of the horse. It would spook him. He'd leap away to the end of the rope from the snubbing post and hop about on three legs. When he calmed down he was spooked again, and so it went on, sometimes hours and sometimes days, until the horse no longer took notice and could be touched by the slicker all over his body.

This "sacking out" was an important education. A rider working horseback cussed a horse that was "goosy," "spooky," or shied when unexpected objects brushed by or touched him. Such a horse was not only a nuisance, but dangerous. If a rider were thrown from a horse that had suddenly spooked and bucked, he was often left afoot with miles between him and the camp or home ranch.

After the sacking lesson, the horse's leg was again tied up, a blanket and saddle were ushered onto the horse's back, and the cinch was gradually tightened. Ideally, the bronc might be saddled and unsaddled fifty or more times until he stood as unconcerned as an old cow horse. A few days later the bronc buster lifted himself into the stirrup, getting the horse used to the feel of weight on the saddle. He might even wait until the horse appeared bored with this stepping into and out of the stirrup before he eased himself into the saddle. Then the rope holding up the leg was released. The horse probably walked quietly, if awkwardly, around the corral, and might not even attempt to buck. Now green broke, the horse was turned into the remuda or to a cowboy who continued with the horse's education.

Some bronc men considered this "nice and easy" technique the ideal way, but not all agreed. Nor were some of the broncs so easily gentled.

Somewhere in the folkways of the sailor it was said that a calm sea never made a mariner. Neither did a gentle horse make a man a bronc rider.

It was a sixth sense that enabled a wild horse rider to earn his living; not only to stay on, but—when he felt a fall coming—to kick the stirrups free, go limp, and roll relaxed after hitting the ground. Learning how to leave a horse was just as important as learning how to stay on. But when the twisting gyrations came too forcefully and the rider's torso turned rubbery and his head started snapping back and forth, he knew he'd lost the round. At that moment nothing loomed more dreadful in his mind than being tossed while having a foot hung in the stirrup. A man could be dragged and kicked to death.

If a wild horse proved to be "dynamite" a bronc man might tie the stirrups together under the horse's belly to aid his own leg control. Or he might use a bucking roll: a slicker or coat tied behind the saddle horn to help wedge him in the saddle.

There were other gimmicks for the "just too salty" broncs, as when a rider dampened his chaps with water to prevent slipping in the saddle. Or he might take a hitch on the horse's tail and whirl him around until the horse was dizzy. Momentarily the horse would lose his will to fight and could be easily mounted.

Even the purist bronc man, who despised these cheating ways and relied on his prowess and pride to stay aboard, might have to hedge his chances if a horse proved too salty to ride. In those days no one man could cope with all the extensive acrobatics of the old time wild horse. There were many.

A "gut twister" was a horse with snake-like contortions. But a blind bucker was driven to panic when mounted. He'd crash a corral or hit a tree head-on. This type covered a lot of ground. One Nevada cowboy named Harry Mays rode a big bay horse after it had been roughed out by a bronc man. Harry was riding in a large corral when the horse began bucking and squealing "to beat sixty." The horse pounded into the gate, breaking the latch, and the gate then swung open. The horse reeled back and fell. Harry quickly abandoned the horse, then leaped to secure the gate before the horse stampeded out. As he looked back to check on the horse he noticed it lying still. It was dead.[9]

A "pile driver" burst into a series of leaps interrupted by stiff-legged landings on all fours. It caused earthquakes in a man's innards. Frequently the pounding caused the man to hemorrhage from the mouth and nose. The pile driver term had nothing to do with machinery, but because the concussions could "pound one's hemorrhoids right up between the shoulder blades."

The horse that was a "cloud hunter" wasn't difficult to ride, but he might fall over backwards. This bronc reared wildly, vaulted upward, and pawed the air with his forefeet. He easily lost his balance, putting the rider on an anxious alert, ready to bail off if he felt that the horse had reared back too far ever to land on his front feet again.

"Weaving" and "sunfishing" were devastating maneuvers that tended to come from the orneriest broncs. A weaver relied on a snakelike motion. His hooves never struck the ground in a straight line while bucking. Ramon Adams called it a bucking style "most disconcerting to a rider."[10]

A sunfisher was worse. He would leap into the air and then turn sideways until his hooves pointed skyward. Just before landing he straightened his body to land on all fours. For most riders that was cutting close to disaster. Many voluntarily threw themselves out of the saddle.

An old range adage about broncs said "there was never a horse that couldn't be rode, or a rider that couldn't be throwed." The bronc that was a "spinner" gave little credence to the first part of the saying and a lot of truth to the second. The spinner bucked two or three jumps then spun into a tight, whirling spin, right or left. Only the horse's agility and speed determined how long a bronc man stayed in the saddle. A combination of vertigo and centrifugal force propelled the bronc man into the air, and "the next thing he remembers," said Will James, "is shaking his head—trying to get back among the living." Only some broncs' inability to sustain a whirling pattern prevented them from being unridable.

The average cowboy detested bucking in horses. But bucking was a trait of the wild horse, and some spirited displays had to be accepted as part of the hazard of being a rider. A cowboy never knew when a horse might break into a fit of bucking. Sometimes he'd start when the saddle was thrown on him. Others were a little more sporting and waited until the rider settled into the saddle. Sometimes, out of a most leisurely mood, the horse would buck into a spasm as if he had deliberately lured his rider into half-guardedness.

Ed Hanks told about such a horse called Jack Dempsey. This bay belonged to the Double Square horse outfit in Paradise Valley, owned by John Taylor and Jim Edson. They ran horses all over that part of northern Nevada and into Oregon and Idaho. Neither of them knew how many horses they actually owned. Each fall they would gather a thousand head, however, to meet market demands.

Ed had never seen anybody ride the beautiful bay. When he asked Edson why, Edson replied, "That's Jack Dempsey, he bucks his man off every year; he's got kind of a bad name around here."

Ed requested permission to ride the horse. All went well for quite a while, but one day, said Ed,

> after we had run mustangs all morning, we tied up our horses and went into the shade by the chuck wagon to eat. When we got through eating I untied Jack Dempsey and got on. We were quite close to the chuck wagon, and that horse shot right up into the air. He kicked dust into all the pots and kettles, and made the cook real mad. He tried every trick he knew and he knew a lot of them, but when he finally got through I was still there. I think it kind of surprised him, and when I got off of him I teased him. I wasn't mad at him.
>
> "So that's the way you buck a man off," I said, "you surprise him after a hard morning, no wonder you got yourself a bad name." He never bucked with me after that, and he was a real good horse. I used him for running mustangs.[11]

Most range horsemen, bronc busters and cowboys, agree that the stallion was the most difficult to break and the saltiest to ride. Al Erwin said of his experiences with Nevada mustangs in the 1920s:

> The first thing they think about is shedding everything that they are not accustomed to. . . . They have a tendency to run and buck constantly, turning their head from side to side, biting the rider in the legs, falling over him, always thinking about getting away, even if it means taking the rider with him. They don't stop for ditches, fences, gullies, or obstacles of any kind, which seems to me indicative of their surefootedness. They have been known to strike you with their front feet or bite you with all their might like a wild animal.[12]

Stallions weren't preferred as working ranch horses, and virtually all ranches castrated their male horses before they were turned into a rider's string. Mustangers, however, rarely had the time. One breaker tried to buck out mustang studs by tying a dummy, with shirt, pants, and jacket to the saddle. The horse bucked for a moment, then suddenly stopped when it felt no reaction from the rider. Some of the studs would stick their heads into the sagebrush and just stand there. "I never could figure that out," Ed Hanks told me.

While most cowboys loathed bucking, they did accept what Will James felt: "I wouldn't give 'two bits' for a bronc that didn't buck when first rode, 'cause I figger it's their mettle showing when they do. It's the right spirit at the right time."

Most riders would accept a mild bucking from their horses on a cold morning, to loosen up their muscles—so long as the horse quit soon afterwards. An outlaw bucker was something else.

These broncs who shed everything but their skin were frequently man-made by a bronc fighter who gave little attention to the nature of the horse he was breaking. Horses that were hot-blooded, nervous and excitable, required careful handling. Others were jug-headed and needed a lot of pulling around. Handling the former in the way of the latter could create outlaws. They would fight with awesome intensity whenever a man climbed aboard. These broncs never lasted as part of a ranch remuda. Invariably they ended up where bucking was a virtue, in a Wild West Show or Bucking Horse Contest.

iii

The Elko Stampede was one of the famous rodeos of the West. Its bronco horses, spoiled ranch horses and mustangs from the hills, drew the best contestants. So did the name of Guadalupe Garcia, whose hand-made saddles, spurs, and bits were offered as prizes. Garcia ran the most colorful saddle shop west of the Rockies and gave Elko's three-day Labor Day festivities priority to dozens of itinerant contest riders.

Garcia was born in San Luis Obispo, California, in 1864, a product of the last days of the Spanish pastoral life. In the coastal valleys and the chaparral hills he lived the life of a vaquero. But the smell of leather went deeper with him, and eventually he preferred the art of saddle making. After an apprenticeship at a San Luis Obispo saddle firm, and a partnership in a saddle shop at Santa Margarita, Garcia decided to come to Elko, Nevada, and open his own saddle store. He had heard about Elko from buckaroos who had trailed their stock to the California coast for winter grazing. (This was before the practice of raising hay for winter feed.) Along with Winnemucca, Elko was a major cattle shipping point. Since the 1880s cattle were trailed from all over the state and from Idaho to the railhead at Elko. From there Nevada beef went to stock markets at Omaha and Chicago.

In 1893, on Thanksgiving Day, Garcia arrived in Elko with two suitcases of rawhide and silver work, and a bride. He could not have found a better locale for his saddle shop. Buckaroos and vaqueros, particular about their riding equipment which was part of their every moment as riders, found in the Garcia products the best craftsmanship in leather and bit and spur work. Many horsemen eventually proclaimed they could not sit their saddle horse easily if not on a Garcia-made saddle.

He set up his shop in the livery stable of the Mayer Hotel, now the Stockman's Hotel. By 1903 he had issued his first catalog. In 1904 he won the gold medal at the World's Fair in St. Louis, and in the following year his saddle craftsmanship took another prize at the Lewis and Clark Exposition in Portland, Oregon. All the leather in this prize saddle was hand-stamped and mounted with gold, silver, and diamonds. The silver was hand-fitted and engraved and was valued at $5,000. Today, protected by a vault in Reno, the saddle is worth $50,000.

Soon Garcia saddles were traveling to Mexico, Canada, Australia, Argentina, and even France. The exports to France were by way of French sheepmen living as herders in Nevada. Later, when they returned to France, the feel of a Garcia saddle was too much a part of them. They took the saddles with them and later sent for more.

Garcia was also the founding and ruling spirit of the Elko Rodeo. No man loved more the excitement of men and horses and cattle, and he gave Elko its most colorful decades.

Buckaroos from all over the West came; sheepherders and miners, businessmen and ranchers to celebrate the gala holiday. Elko itself donned the holiday aura in posters and banners. Bars, restaurants, and hotels teemed with people who came for the rodeo and also to gape at the prize saddles and silver inlaid spurs offered by Garcia for the top contestants. But Garcia made sure that the riders earned these prizes.

Weeks before the rodeo, Garcia advertised in the *Elko Independent* for wild horses. The advertisement was a brisk one:

ELKO STAMPEDE
Bucking Horses Wanted

We will give $10.00 in cash to the owners of outlaw horses for every time one of our riders is thrown at the BIG STAMPEDE IN ELKO—September 1 to 3, 1913.

Feed bills while here at our expense.

Horses bought at the end of the stampede if they are mean enough and can buck.

Bring in your bucking horses and get a little

EASY MONEY.
G. S. Garcia[13]

Ten dollars for every time a horse threw a cowboy was good inducement for mustangers, cowboys, and Indians to scout the hills and valleys rounding up wild horses. The *Elko Independent* recorded the proceedings with journalistic glee:

> G. S. Garcia has received the wildest horse in America for the Elko Stampede on Labor Day. This horse is the ugliest, most ferocious one now in captivity. It nearly chewed an Indian up over in Eureka, and will be a feature for the big stampede.[14]

Another news item reported that all the horses were mean, and that they were known as the worst in the country. One was so mean that it lay down and died soon after reaching Elko.[15]

Others were mean enough to be remembered to this day. Movin' Picture, a small horse caught in Pine Valley, was a headliner from 1913 to 1915. Then there were Bill Hell, Sometimes (sometimes you rode him, sometimes you didn't), Bold Hornet, Hell's Descent, Black Demon, and so on.

Garcia often bought the best buckers from the cowboys. Some he probably traded to the Pendleton or Calgary stampede, which in that day owned their strings of horses and were always searching for the toughest to headline their rodeos. Eastern buyers also came to Elko for horses, looking for possible polo ponies from the wild herds. A horse had to be tough for the polo sport, and the mustang, once trained, had the "spirit and ginger" for polo pony qualifications. One agent followed the rodeo circuit and purchased outstanding horses for the British Polo Club, which liked the hardy, tough make-up of Nevada mustangs.[16]

iv

They were also "sweet riding horses," and for many Nevadans, capturing a mustang for riding or driving was a common affair. Sometimes an Indian or cowboy would take to the hills and bring back a mustang for a client. Five dollars for the effort was the usual price.

A sudden demand for many wild horses often commenced when a mineral strike or boom vibrated out of some isolated part of Nevada. The rush to the strike and the enormous demands made for goods and equipment necessitated an army of horses. Often there weren't enough, and some cowboys made a lucrative business rounding up wild horses and breaking them for teamsters, stagecoach lines, and individuals looking vainly for some mode of transportation to the field.

Johnny O'Keefe, a youthful and talented stage driver, may not be typical, but he is one of the more interesting entrepreneurs. Johnny started the triweekly Tonopah Stage out of Sodaville just after the greatest boom of the twentieth century began in Tonopah. Before Jim Butler made his find, the Tonopah region was a quiet land, part of the immense Nevada desert. Cattle grazed the land, and herders would pass their sheep through on their way to one of the northern valleys for summer grazing. The nearest railhead was sixty miles away at Sodaville on the Carson and Colorado Railroad. When the news of Butler's find at Tonopah came over the wires, small, unassuming Sodaville found itself swamped with people and tons of equipment to be freighted over the desert.

Johnny's stage line departed Sodaville upon arrival of the C&C at nine in the morning. He arrived with his passengers in Tonopah about nine that evening. The sixty-mile bumpy, dusty jaunt was relieved with rest stops at Crow Springs and Millers.

Still the people came, and Johnny expanded his line to a daily run between Sodaville and Tonopah. By now horsepower had priced itself threefold as freighting demands caused a scarcity of horses. But wild horses were in abundance at nearby Pilot Mountain, Smoky Valley, and Candalaria, and cowboys were more than willing to run the mustangs for use in Johnny's stage line for five dollars a head.

Johnny, however, didn't have much time for breaking. Vacant slots were always occurring in his six-ups as horses took on injuries and his number of stagecoaches increased. So "Hook 'em up!" was his command, wild as they were.

Lilly Pepper, who lived in Sodaville at the time of the Tonopah boom, told me, "Even to this day I'll never know how they ever harnessed those horses. They were green as gourds! It used to be a ritual to stand at the Lathrop and Davis General Store in anticipation of Johnny thundering his team up to the passenger station, because we knew there would be the antics and fanfare of a new wild horse hitched for the first time. Just minutes before, the horse had been thrown, harnessed, and bridled. Sometimes they made such a commotion at the station people refused to even get into the coach."

Only one wild horse was hitched at a time and always as a near swing. When the stage lunged from the corral area the greenhorn reared and squealed, plunged and grunted, but only to be pushed along by resolute wheelers and leaders. Sometimes, said Lilly Pepper, the frenzied outbursts of the wild horse snapped the harness like a rubber band.[17]

Usually a cowboy rode alongside the wild horse with a trip rope attached in case the wild one became unmanageable. After the first rest stop fifteen miles from Sodaville, the wild horse was exhausted and foam-lathered. If the horse showed that he had accepted his lot he would be exchanged with the rest of the team. If he still showed fight he stayed hitched until the next stop another fifteen miles away.

When Johnny's stage arrived back in Sodaville, people speculated on the probability of the wild horse having made it. Most of the horses did, a little thinner, but docile and conditioned to their role. Some, no doubt, were not so fortunate. And so it went until the railroad connected with Tonopah.

Hauling mail, parcel post, and supplies to isolated mountain towns was frequently done by mustang teams. Cheapness, expendability, and hardiness made the wild horse ideal. The mountain town of Jarbidge in northern Nevada required tough horses to plow and wedge their way through heavy snowpacks to deliver wagon supplies. Half the horses used were green mustangs, some not even halter broke. "That mail route," said one who remembers, "killed off a lot of them."[18]

There has never been a consensus about the merits of the wild horses for domestic uses. There is no denying that they were tough, made good pack horses or wagon pullers, and could literally go forever without tiring. Opinions diverge, however, on their worth as riding mounts. Some did extol the wild horse; others felt that as ranch horses, where hours would have to be spent on their backs, they fatigued a rider. "They would kill you," reflected Dominique Laxalt who rode them when packing grub to remote sheep camps in Nevada. "They get you in the kidneys with their short walking. Shake you to pieces."

Jewell Martin, who formerly ranched in Northern Nevada,

is of the same opinion, but only regarding the smaller wild horses found in the desert. "Their gaits were choppy and shook you to fatigue. In the northern part of the state the wild ones were a huskier, bigger type, and in some ways they were the best; surefooted and knew every nook and cranny and never got caught in a badger hole because they had run wild in that part of the country."[19]

Mostly, Jewell liked them for their endurance and speed. He enjoyed racing horses, and one he caught wild on Beaver Creek was always a winner as long as it raced in the Jarbidge Fourth of July celebrations. The horse was known as the Beaver Creek mustang.

"Back then," says Jewell, "about 1915, we had all sorts of races during holiday celebrations—foot races, sack races, men's races, women's races, kids' races—but it was the horse races that brought people from Salt Lake and from Idaho to match horses for a quarter of a mile down Jarbidge's main street. The prize was a hundred dollars, fifty dollars in cash and a fifty dollar prize. Hundreds more were wagered. A lot of good horses were brought to the races, but that Beaver Creek mustang never lost a race, and that was when we raced three heats—two out of three declared the winner. That mustang had that quick power surge to carry him over the finish line first every time. There were a lot of poor mustangs, but a good one just couldn't be beat for any use."

Al Erwin, one of those sorely addicted horse lovers who rode all kinds as a cowboy, felt that when wild horses were handled gently you won their affection and confidence. Afterwards, he said, one could not wish for a more faithful, dependable, surefooted cow horse.

Until recently Melvin Jones, a rancher out in Pine Valley, converted mustangs to cow ponies with enormous success. "We used to find some good ones in the wild herds, those with the conformation able to do the job. Many were built just right; could get their feet under them and had style and speed. Of course the look of intelligence counts, too. Conformation and intelligence: these add up to making a good athlete which is what any cow horse must be whether born wild or ranch bred."

Jones trained wild horses for ranch work, for pleasure, and for competition in major shows against quarter horses, Morgans and Thoroughbreds. A horse named Smartie was his best. He was a two-year-old when he was herded into a corral by a plane in 1948 out of the rough and broken country south of Battle Mountain in the Antelope Valley.

Jones liked the particular look of the young stallion. He wasn't big, but quick, alert, and showed intelligence. Jones named the horse Smartie and started working stock on him, getting in miles of ranch and cow work which Jones feels is important for developing strength, balance, and ability.

When Smartie was four years old Jones showed him at the 1951 Elko County Horse Show. Against tough competition in which many top stock horses were tested, Smartie took first in two classes. Jones didn't bother with too much showing after Elko. He was a working rancher and that had priority. Smartie continued to develop into a fine cow horse, however, and when he was eight years old, Jones trailered him to the Cow Palace at San Francisco for the Olympics of the reined cow-horse competition. All other horses were registered quarter horses manned by professional trainers. After eliminations, Smartie was one of seventeen in the final competition. He humiliatingly defeated the sixteen other contestants and became champion cow horse for that year.

Of course, Smartie was exceptional. The most appealing aspect of most Nevada mustangs was simply their low price. Horse dealers found quick markets for the Nevada wild horse on farms and dude ranches, with pack horse outfits, and as cheap riding transportation. This last attraction brought one horse dealer from Buffalo, Kentucky, to Nevada on annual buying sprees. Usually he shipped six or eight carloads of wild horses back to Kentucky.

"A poor man in my state," he declared, "cannot afford to buy the horses raised there which sell from $150 to $600 each. The Nevada horses that I ship will bring an average price of $30 to $50 which are purchased by people of small means. You know, we have more common people than common horses in Kentucky."[20]

7

The Horse Nobody Wants

Historically, wild horses have been a nuisance on the range, and historically, cattlemen have been wild horses' arch enemy. They have shot at, poisoned, chased, and captured wild horses. Cattlemen claimed that wild horse herds harassed cattle, broke water troughs, trampled water holes, and lured domestic horses into the wild way of life. The worst offense of all: they ate the grass.

Ranchers' attacks thickened when cattle prices rose and wild horses took range feed that could support more cows. When cattle prices—or the horse prices—plummeted, as they always did, ranchers increased the numbers of loose running horses by turning out saddle and work stock to forage for themselves. Rarely were they reclaimed.

The low points of these economic spasms did most to create

the vast herds in Nevada, southern Oregon, Idaho, Utah, and Washington during the first decades of the twentieth century, long after wild horses had ceased to be a problem east of the Rocky Mountains. Although the rough-hewn mountain lands of the arid West were not the most favorable environment in some respects, the many canyons and cul-de-sac hideouts provided havens for numerous herds against recurrent onslaughts.

The increase in herds worsened the range which had already deteriorated under massive sheep migrations. Then, too, trucks and tractors were eclipsing work horses, which were being turned loose to live in the hills.

Montana, for example, apparently had no wild horse problem until after World War I when wheat farmers abandoned their horses for steam threshers. (These horses and their descendants became a rich source for pet food manufacturers in the 1920s.) Ironically, just a few years before, in 1913, Montana had felt confident that the few herds roaming free had been captured. That roundup with its resolute fifty-mile effort to capture every last horse became nationwide news. A cowboy was stationed for nearly every mile of the chase, taking up the pursuit as another cowboy's horse fell out from fatigue. The wild bunch, said the report, was literally run off its feet. The herd leader, a jet-black stallion, was finally found maimed and bleeding after running into a barbed wire fence. He was shot.[1]

The business of living has never been easy for the wild horse. In the Great Basin there were always horses about, like the sagebrush, and some men schemed to utilize these useless commodities to commercial advantage.

Wild horses proved, if sporadically, more easily convertible to profit than sagebrush to balms and hair oils. In 1899 a new Nevada industry was heralded when a man named Benson, "a capitalist from Bangor, Maine," opened a cannery and tannery plant at Mud Lake near Pyramid Lake, north of Reno. Benson paid horse hunters seventy-five cents for the saddle and hindquarters of wild horses and fifty cents for their hides delivered at the tannery.

The meat was boiled in a hot spring near the plant, then salted and sealed hermetically, and shipped for human consumption to China, Japan, and the Philippine Islands. Benson was not even held back by Americans' aversion to eating horse meat. Some cans, attractively labeled as wild goat meat, were shipped to Boston's gourmet restaurants.[2] Benson's ruse may have been discovered as there are no later reports of Benson and his wild horse converter plant.

Tannery representatives from outside the state were frequent contractors for Nevada's wild horses. Reports as early as 1897 tell of hide buyers contracting for horsehides in the heavily horse-populated counties of Eureka, Nye, and Lander. One buyer contracted for two thousand hides, paying $1.80 a hide and three cents a pound for mane and tails.[3]

For the most part such enterprises were haphazard in their early stages. Much depended on the men who hunted down the horses. Most of them were buckaroos who took on the distasteful job when ranch work was in ebb. Many quit with guilt feelings after shooting a few horses. Others indulged only to the extent of earning enough money to hold them over until ranch work demanded them. Consequently, no large enough dents in the wild herds were made to alleviate the concern of ranchers. Until the federal government became involved with the removal of feral horses, the problem remained a millstone for local ranchers and regional stockmen's associations.

In 1899 Nevada lawmakers passed the first wild horse legislation which encouraged shooting wild horses and marketing their hides. The law was repealed at the following legislative session, because the hides of too many branded horses were appearing at eastern stock yards. Stockmen then adopted a resolution requesting the legislature to pass a law allowing the U.S. Forest Service to shoot wild horses on the forest preserves. Here prime summer range remained for cattle and sheep, and protecting it from wild horses was considered imperative.

Apparently, no immediate action was taken. But on February 19, 1908, two news stories datelined Reno, and carried over a national wire, stated:

> A campaign to exterminate wild horses in the Toyabe [*sic*], Toquima, and Monitor forest preserves in Lander County has been started, and it is believed that more than fifteen thousand wild horses now grazing on these preserves will be slaughtered before another year has passed. . . . These horses destroy the vegetation and do much harm to the entire district, consequently a war of extermination will be waged against them.

The other stated:

> The forestry department at Washington has ordered the rangers to kill all wild horses on the government domain.[4]

W. C. Barnes, a dedicated early forestry official, reported the public reactions to the news releases:

> One tender-hearted individual called it an outrage to kill so valuable an animal when it could be used for the benefit of man.
>
> A firm of hide dealers wrote asking to be given a contract for the sole handling of the hides taken from the slaughtered horses. A large manufacturing company wanted to purchase all the hides, for use in making certain kinds of leather goods. Another firm inquired if the animals were to be killed at some central point; if so, could they not arrange to utilize the flesh of these animals for canning purposes?
>
> Dozens of men wrote offering to go to Nevada and capture the animals if the Government would pay their fare out and give them the horses in return for their work. One man wrote from Texas, "If the men that issued that order knew anything about the nature and habits of the Western mustang, they would know it was a very easy matter to capture them. If the Government will employ me at a salary of $100 per month, I will agree to gather all in three months."

> Another group of correspondents, mostly Eastern lads with a desire for adventure, wrote to obtain employment as "horse-killers," announcing themselves as dead shots with a rifle and expert hunters of game.
>
> A member of the Humane Society demanded that a more humane method than shooting be employed.[5]

Letters protesting the government action were probably in the majority, repeating a similar public outcry of some years before when it was suggested by a spokesman for the forest service that the Army might combine target practice with wild horse eradication.[6]

To all letters the forest service replied that no orders were issued for the killing of wild horses in the national forests. The report, the forest service further stated, "originated in an unwarranted press dispatch given out through the newspapers of the country."

This was double talk. There was no doubt that the long war against Nevada's wild horses had begun.

ii

Four major markets rose in the 1920s which caused a significant and permanent decline in feral horses on the western ranges. Neither the least nor most significant of these outlets, but a constant siphoner of wild horses until 1970 was the chicken-feed processor. Processing plants at Vernon, Petaluma, and Haywood, all in California, paid a top price of five dollars a head for mature horses while yearlings sold for $2.50. Any colts accompanying their mares were gratis.

The prices paid were high, a strong inducement for organized efforts to supply range horses for chicken raisers. Processors could afford the payments after working out an agreement with the railroad which reduced shipping rates to the plants by designating such horses as chicken feed. As a result, railroads were under no legal obligation to give humane treatment to the horses.[7] They were crowded tightly into boxcars for their long and sluggish freight ride to the rendering plants. It was unlikely that the horses were watered as too many man hours would have been required to unload, water, and then reload them.

How many wild range horses made this ride to the plants is almost impossible to determine. But scores of small press items in Nevada newspapers throughout the twenties and thirties attest that thousands were shipped to California. A typical news item, usually accompanied by an editorial comment, went like this:

> Two hundred head of wild horses which have been running on the range in the vicinity of Mary's River feeding on the forage which should be left for cattle and doing nothing but damage to the entire country will be shipped from Deeth to Petaluma, California, in the near future, where they will be used for chicken feed.[8]

Probably the largest single shipment of horses (six thousand head) went out from Elko, Nevada, in 1925. This consignment required a special train on the Western Pacific to transport the horses to Petaluma.[9]

While West Coast poultry farmers had a reasonably cheap source of foodstuff in the wild horses, the industry absorbed only a small fraction of the horses running wild. In 1924 the pet food industry edged into the market. This industry became the chief reason for draining wild horses off the range during the extensive roundups of the 1920s.

The firm of Chappel Brothers of Rockford, Illinois, became both famous and infamous as the first and major convertor of wild horses for the food dishes of America's most beloved pets. By 1935 when Americans were spending about forty million dollars annually on dog and cat food,[10] Chappel Brothers were the significant provider of horse meat for pets. The firm also packed "clods" of horse meat for human consumption in Holland, Norway, and other Scandinavian countries.[11]

Chappel Brothers purchased their horses for as low as

$1.50 to $2.00 a head. Most of them were coming off the ranges in Montana and Wyoming where cowboys under direct Chappel hire rode the former Indian lands capturing wild horses and buying reprobates of no apparent use to anyone except Chappel. There were periods when the firm was slaughtering five to seven hundred horses a day.[12] In 1928, forty thousand horses were converted for pet food and for export to Europe.[13]

Business may be business, but somehow the idea of killing horses has always been repugnant to many. Chappel Brothers was constantly besieged by threats and accusations that the horses awaiting slaughter in the corrals were not being fed. Various investigations by a humane society failed, however, to prove the allegations. One of Chappel's riders stated that the horses were in fact well fed and that it was the nature of wild horses, when penned up, to kick and bite (this had been interpreted as hunger by the overly-concerned)[14].

Another irritant to Chappel was a horse-loving cowboy who tried to dynamite the plant, after other unsuccessful attempts at arson and cutting high power lines into the plant. "I couldn't help it," he pleaded in court. "I am a cowboy and I love horses. I can't bear to think of people eating them." He was declared insane.[15]

Chappel finally enclosed the slaughterhouse with a high, barbed wire fence and strangers were forbidden to enter the premises.

The economic success of Chappel Brothers encouraged others to enter the business. By 1928 four firms were in operation. Two plants, in Oregon and Montana, were using only wild horses. Another, back East, was converting old and worn dray horses to canned food. In California the Ross Dog and Cat Food Company, the largest plant on the West Coast, received its horses from Nevada, Arizona, Utah, and New Mexico.

For a while the business was lucrative. But it was a precarious enterprise which relied on keeping the price of horses low and the flow of herds into the plants steady. Disenchantment, not only because of competition for the horses, but because of irate impulses from concerned horse lovers, weakened some of those in the business. A reporter for *Cattleman* magazine, published in Texas, wrote this graphic account in 1928 of a visit to a Far West slaughterhouse:

> My letter admitted me to an outer office. A round, immaculate, worried looking man with red cheeks came to where I waited and said he was the head of the business. He said also, and with considerable emphasis, that he was sick of it; that there wasn't any money in it and there wasn't any future to it. Cranks wrote you letters, he said, and sentimental old women came sniffing around and reporters kept coming and distorting what you told them into outrageous lies.

When the reporter asked how many horses went through the plant in a year he was answered:

> Nothing like as many as people said. The most ever to be killed in a week was nine hundred and this week, for instance, not one. That's how it went. You never knew what to count on. A rotten business. . . . The horse meat business was on the skids. . . . It was being overdone.

Later the reporter watched a string of boxcars being unloaded. He said that 18 cars, with about 25 miserable, bedraggled horses to a car—some 450 head in all—were herded into a corral. A railroad man looked at the reporter: "They keep 'em coming," he said disgustedly. "Whyn't they just kill them where they are?"[16]

Processing of horses reached its peak in 1933 when 29,610,381 pounds of horse meat were canned.[17] As horse numbers diminished some firms went out of business while others reverted to other animals and byproducts from livestock houses to feed America's cats and dogs.

Meanwhile, under orders of the secretary of Agriculture, a determined effort to rid the national forests of all wild horses was being pursued. In 1928 high-powered rifles were brought into the plan and hunters went into the hills to shoot horses. This time it was not to be a casual activity merely to cut down on the numbers of horses, but outright extermination.

At first the government offered a bounty of fifty cents a head, which was later raised to $1.50 a head. One hunter in the Toiyabe National Forest in northern Nevada brought down eight hundred head in one year. By 1928 only nine horses were known to be at large, and these were to be shot also. Virtually all of the two thousand horses known to be living in the Toiyabe Forest range had been exterminated.[18] Nor has the horse ever again been allowed to encroach on this national forest and others throughout the West, although small numbers probably do exist today.

iii

The greatest blow to the feral horse, one with sledge hammer devastation, came with the passage of the Taylor Grazing Act by the Congress in 1934.

All public land laws enacted prior to the Taylor act had converted public lands to private ownership, as with the homestead acts. Once settlements moved west of the Great Plains and into the Great Basin areas, the acreage allowance for homesteading was not sufficient to provide adequate grazing because of the low carrying capacity of some of the public lands. Consequently the allotment was increased to 640 acres.

Some applicants actually had no intention to homestead, but to gain access to or control vast open tracts of public grazing lands.[19] This area of abuse has to be explored to better understand the deterioration of the range which led to the Taylor Grazing Act and the removal of horses from the range.

Shortly after cattle ranching became established, with considerable capital investment in buildings, corrals, and riders, sheep wedged into the range in competition with cattle for grass and other range plants. Sheep herding was mobile and required little capital investment. A burro or two, or a sheepwagon for the herder's supplies, and a couple of dogs accompanied sheep bands as they trailed hundreds of miles while feeding. Often they ate their way through winter ranges in Nevada and then back to the mountain country of California, Oregon, and Idaho for summer grazing and raising lambs. This winter range was sometimes on land adjacent to cattle ranches, leaving little for cattle to feed on during critical periods in the grazing seasons.

To the chagrin of cattlemen, bankers encouraged sheep herding. Profits were greater than with cattle and risk was considerably less. Later, when land laws were converting public lands into private ownership, many itinerant sheep herders filed on 640 acre tracts in good grazing areas, but used that filing only as an opportunity to graze surrounding lands. Rarely was any attempt made to improve upon the land. At the termination of the three-year period allowed for making proof through improvements, many sheepmen relinquished their claims.

Along with periods of drought, prime parcels of land were passing out of the public domain thus putting more stress on the diminishing public lands. The range decayed rapidly. Cattlemen blamed sheepmen, sheepmen blamed cattlemen, and often both blamed the useless tramp horses. But few seemed ready to admit what E. R. Jackman, an Oregon range specialist knew: that if every plant has to fight for existence, "any use at all is, in a sense, overuse."

Finally, the blow from the 1929 depression shattered the livestock business into virtual bankruptcy (it had been declining for some years). But cattlemen now listened to a new, major concept for the administration of public lands. The Taylor Grazing Act[20] established grazing districts to be used by stockmen for a nominal fee. The act also limited the number of livestock to the carrying capacity of particular ranges. Most cattlemen accepted the new policy with its restrictions. A few resented government interference, as did the sheepmen, who opposed any restrictions on grazing.

Horsemen, particularly those who ran horses on the range or utilized wild horses for markets, prepared to fight the government when it declared unbranded horses as useless range tramps. These horsemen believed that having their horses loose on the range would guarantee range rights for them. And although it was admitted that the demand for horses had slipped drastically after World War I, there was still enough young stock of better quality to serve a market for saddle and stock horses. The poorer horses could always be sold for chicken feed.

No one knows how many "back in the hills" horse breeders—those usually living in a shack and owning hundreds of horses out on the range—made some sort of living selling bunches of horses now and then. There were more than the government realized, however, and they filtered into every town courthouse in Nevada, Idaho, and Oregon to fight the government edict. Their vociferous resentment of the government's interference with private enterprise created the major news in both small town weeklies and the dailies at state capitals.

If the government argued the old range adage that "a horse will eat twice as much as a cow on the range," horsemen replied that "a horse will live where a cow will die." When the government contended that a better class of horses could be produced by taking away the culls and introducing better stallions, horse raisers countered that those range areas where the horses were roaming were incapable of producing better range animals than already found there. And besides, they added, introducing better horses would require a considerable investment.

In its final statement the government contended that the Taylor Grazing Act was passed for range management. Unbranded or unclaimed domestic horses running loose were a threat to that management program and would have to go. The initial step in the government's program for removing all these horses was public notice announcing a specific area of the public range from which horses were to be removed. The notice allowed sufficient time for horse owners to withdraw their branded stock. Those remaining would be captured and impounded. Any branded stock that was captured could be redeemed by its owner if he paid a proportionate share of the expenses incurred by the government in capturing and feeding the animals.

Two points of the program went awry: First, the men contracted by the government had only minor success in capturing the really wild horses, those born to the life. Second, resentment by some horsemen made them work overtime to circumvent the government action. These owners rounded up all the horses they could gather and held them in pasture until the government men had captured what was left. When the time period for a particular area had elapsed, the horses held on pasture were turned loose. Almost as many horses were again running free as before the government started its eradication program.

The government decided to get tougher. This time, with the consent and backing of permittees using the range, mostly cattlemen, the government issued orders closing a range to horse grazing. In addition to the public notice, individuals with horses out on the range were notified by registered mail to claim their horses. Those left on the range would be shot.

Closing a range indefinitely could only mean enormous expense for those willing to hold their horses in pasture and feed them hay. And the muscle talk of shooting horses was quickly challenged. But a precedent had recently been established in a federal court in Arizona. Two branded horses loose on the Sitgreaves National Forest range were shot after notices to remove the horses had been announced by the government. Two federal employees were arrested (after having been roughed up by indignant private parties) and charged by local officials with shooting privately owned horses. The government applied for an injunction through the federal court to restrain county officials from interfering with the program in the national forests. The case rested on the question whether branded horses could be classified as wild. The judge ruled that a horse could be wild, even though branded.[21]

The sledge hammer had fallen, and the government now pursued unhampered extermination of the feral horse. Thousands were taken off the ranges. In Wyoming, between 1936 and 1940, about four thousand head were removed. Oregon estimated in 1940 that about a thousand unbranded horses still ran wild after ten thousand had been swept away.

In parts of Nevada, horses held their own. Northern Elko County, with its rough mountain hideouts, hindered efforts to extricate the horses. Much of the rest of northern Nevada also had a low percentage of removal. Farther south, where desert flats predominate, the removal was almost complete and horses no longer were considered a range problem.[22]

Bitterness still lingers with old-time range men who gave up their horses under pressure from the government. Some, admitting the necessity for the action, felt that the government was brutal in the way they handled the removal. One individual in Elko County remembers a light government plane chasing herds off a bluff four hundred feet high.[23] Others resented the attitude of Taylor grazing men who bluntly warned certain ranchers to remove their horses, "for when the killing starts we won't be looking for brands."[24]

Conversely, officials of the Taylor program had their patience frayed raw by horse owners who cheated and harassed members of the Taylor act program. Even after the law had settled into routine, and resentment was losing much of its force, some individuals continued to undermine the program. One agent, knowing that a particular individual had a permit to graze two hundred horses in the northeastern part of Nevada, was aware that many more than the allotted number of horses were on the range. The agent advised the rancher to clean up his area. Sometime later, under government supervision, that particular rancher's herds were corralled; 3,700 head were counted and only 1,178 were branded. The rancher was fined nearly eight thousand dollars in trespass fines.[25]

This instance was probably the most flagrant example of abuse of the law. Dozens of smaller but no less irritating instances fill the files of the local Bureau of Land Management office. Often when the government made periodic roundups, branded horses were held in custody until their owners were notified. Meanwhile, the number of horses belonging to particular individuals who had grazing privileges was compared to the number rounded up. Usually those horses in custody outnumbered the permittee's quota. Many owners when thus exposed relinquished claim to the horses rather than pay a trespass fine.[26]

The government did not take possession of these horses permanently. The entire program of clearing up the range was granted to private contractors who did the chasing and capturing. Unbranded horses were given outright to the contractors as were the branded but unclaimed. Some were sold to private buyers while most were shipped to poultry feeders and pet food manufacturers.

Although the man on horseback had been the predominant means of rounding up the mustangs, what had truly doomed the wild horse was the airplane. No canyon could hide a herd from the slow-flying, low-swooping mechanical hawks. Neither could a herd escape once the plane began driving them.

The use of a light aircraft had been proposed and tried previously. As early as 1912 the idea was suggested by an enthusiastic New Yorker to a Nevada mustanger. The air machine, wrote the pilot, can fly high or low, turn quickly in any direction and speed up to sixty miles an hour. The mustanger, too saddle-oriented to concede to the changing mode, wrote in reply that the speed of the pilot's craft was just about the gait necessary to keep up with some of the wild studs.[27]

By the 1930s the use of the plane was no longer occasion for a wry joke. The improved maneuverability of light planes made them very effective. A flyer could move a herd fast or slow. Herd splitting, a defense of horses when chased by horseback, was quickly corrected by a plane. And as long as a herd was heading in the desired direction the plane could circle behind without terrorizing the herd. Once the wild ones reached the corral area, riders took up the chase and funnelled the horses into the corral. Virtually all mustangers admitted that the plane saved a lot of tear on the saddle horses.

By 1940 the last of the great western wild horse roundups was history. One magazine reader reacted to a *Life* magazine photo essay on aerial roundups with the bitter prophecy, "In time to come mayhap some man will take his small son up to a glass case and say, 'Son, that is what was once known as the Western pony.' "[28]

Epilogue

The western mustang of yesterday was a remarkably durable species. Through the centuries, he managed tenaciously to survive the persistent attempts to obliterate him.

Today, his descendant seems assured of existence without undue harassment by man. For the first time, the wild horse has been placed under the far-reaching protection of the federal government.

The problem that remains is one of holding this prolific animal to manageable numbers. The western range must support not only endangered species, but also the cattle and sheep needed to feed and clothe a nation. To compound this situation, public demand for recreational areas is steadily diminishing the open range. The problem will continue to be aggravated.

Inevitably, formulas for use of the range will have to be settled upon between governmental agencies, citizens' groups for preservation of the wild horse, and private ranching interests.

Whatever course the future takes, one fact seems certain. The wild horse—that enduring symbol of the Old West—will be around for a long time to come.

Notes

Chapter One

1. The Spanish-Indian-horse complex has been fastidiously researched and documented. I have drawn freely from numerous sources and synthesized for my purposes.

The introduction of the horse into the Americas and its spread into the northern hemisphere has been a lifetime study of Dr. Francis Haines. Two papers, "Where Did the Plains Indians Get Their Horses" (*American Anthropologist,* January-March, 1938), and "The Northward Spread of Horses Among the Plains Indians" (*American Anthropologist,* July-September, 1938), created new thinking in this area. Dr. Haines's book, *The Appaloosa Horse* (Austin: University of Texas Press, 1963) consolidates and updates his major premises.

Other important sources are D. E. Worcester's "The Spread of Spanish Horses in the Southwest" (*New Mexico Historical Review,* January, 1945); "The Peninsular Background in Latin American Cattle Raising," by Charles J. Bishko (*Hispanic American Review,* November, 1952); and "Did The First Spanish Horses Landed in Florida and Carolina Leave Progeny?" by Thornton Chard (*American Anthropologist,* January-March, 1940).

Canadian scholar Gilbert Frank Roe assesses the mass of information and adds new concepts in his *The Indian and the Horse* (Norman: University of Oklahoma Press, 1955).

For much of the Texas episode on wild horses I am indebted to *Mustangs and Cowhorses,* edited by J. Frank Dobie (Dallas: Southern Methodist University Press, 1965).

The California segment is thoroughly covered in H. H. Bancroft's *California Pastoral* (San Francisco: The History Co., 1888), L. T. Bursham (Sacramento: California Department of Natural Resources, 1957), and Johnnie Walker's "The Wild Horses of Early California" in *Western Horseman* (October, 1936), p. 8.

Chapter Two

1. Bidwell, John, *Echoes of the Past* (New York: Citadel Press, 1962), pp. 51-52.
2. De Quille, Dan, *Washo Rambles* (Los Angeles: Westernlore Press, 1963), p. 107.
3. Simpson, Capt. J. H., *Report of Exploration Across the Great Basin in Utah . . . in 1859* (Washington, D.C.: Government Printing Office, 1876), p. 86.
4. Downs, James F., "Differential Response to White Contact: Paiute and Washo," *The Washo Indians of California and Nevada,* Anthropological Papers no. 67 (Salt Lake City: University of Utah Press, 1963), pp. 125-126.
5. Ewers, John C., *The Horse in Blackfoot Indian Culture* (Washington, D.C.: Bureau of American Ethnology, Bulletin 159, 1955), pp. 33-34.
6. "American" horses have received only sparse attention. The best account is by Paul Albert, "The Romance of the Western Horse," *Western Horseman* (May-June, 1941). Other important mention is made by Herbert S. Auerbach in "Old Trails, Old Forts, Old Trappers and Traders," *Utah Historical Quarterly* (vol. 9, no. 1-2, January-April, 1941), pp. 15-16. Also, Robert H. Fletcher's *Free Grass to Fences, the Montana Range Story* (Helena: Historical Society of Montana, 1960), pp. 95-96.
7. Westgaard, Waldemar, editor and translator, *Denmark and Slesvig (1848-1864), with a collection of illustrated letters by Daniel Bruhn, including his letters from California and Nevada (1864-1872)* (London: Oxford University Press, 1946), pp. 113-120.
8. Interview with Albert Laird, Dayton, Nevada. Also, *Eureka Sentinal,* November 26, 1927.
9. Mills, Lester W., *A Sagebrush Saga* (Springville, Utah: privately printed, 1956), p. 79.
10. Wilson, Joseph W., "Stock Horses of Elko County, Nevada," *Western Horseman* (January-February, 1944).
11. Ibid.
12. Mills, work cited in note 9 above, p. 79.
13. "Wild Mustangs Used in Saddle Horse Breeding," *Eureka Sentinel* (April 21, 1928).
14. "Wild Horses Are Seen Near Reno," *Record Courier* (Gardnerville, June 22, 1928).
15. Lougher, Gregory, "Hunting Wild Horses," *Western Horseman* (November-December, 1937).

16. News item, *Rawhide Rustler* (Rawhide, Nevada, May 9, 1908).

17. Hazeltine, Ben, et al., "A Range History of Nevada," *Western Livestock Journal* (May-June, 1961).

18. Mills, work cited in note 9 above, p. 80.

19. Steele, Rufus, "Mustangs, Busters and Outlaws of the Nevada Wild Horse Country," *American Magazine* (vol. LXXII [1911]), p. 757.

Chapter Three

1. Goldsmith, Walter, "Wild Horses and Outlaws," *Western Horseman* (November-December, 1944, part II), p. 12.

2. Fisher, Mickey, "Mustang Fever," *Western Horseman* (September, 1952), p. 10.

3. Barnes, Will Co., "Wild Horses," *McClure's Magazine* (January, 1909), p. 294.

4. Barnum, Charles, "How I Trap Wild Horses," *Sunset Magazine* (August, 1908), p. 288.

5. Ibid., p. 296.

6. Interview with Jeff Rice, Winnemucca, Nevada.

7. Goldsmith, work cited in note 1 above, p. 12.

8. James, Will, *Cowboys North and South* (New York: Grosset and Dunlap, n.d.), p. 200.

9. "Drugging Nevada's Wild Horses," *Eureka Sentinel* (June 25, 1910).

10. "To Catch Wild Horses," *Elko Weekly Independent* (March 24, 1911).

11. "A Wild Horse Trap," *Elko Weekly Independent* (September 1, 1911).

12. Letter to author from Harry E. Webb, Tujunga, California.

13. Fisher, work cited in note 2 above, p. 10.

14. Arthur, Zua, *Broken Hills* (New York: Vantage Press, 1958), pp. 83-84.

15. Catlin, George, *Letters and Notes on the Manners, Customs, and Conditions of the North American Indians* (London, 1841, vol. VII), pp. 57-60.

16. Collinson, Frank, "Fifty Thousand Mustangs" in *Mustangs and Cowhorses,* edited by J. Frank Dobie (Dallas: Southern Methodist University Press, 1965), p. 75.

17. Goldsmith, Walter, "Wild Horses and Outlaws," *Western Horseman* (September-October, 1944, part I), p. 5.

18. Interview with Ed Hanks, Fallon, Nevada.

19. *Reno Evening Gazette* (February 19, 1897).

20. *Nevada Statutes,* 1897 (Carson City, Nevada: State Printing Office), p. 68.

21. "Horse Killing," *Elko Weekly Independent* (February 4, 1898).

22. Ibid.

23. "Killing Wild Horses, Some Tame Ones Are Missing," *Gardnerville Record* (April 3, 1900).

24. Interview with Jane Riordan, Carson City, Nevada.

25. "Gedney's Wild Horse Bill," *Elko Weekly Independent* (February 10, 1899, February 20, 1899).

26. *Nevada Statutes,* 1901 (Carson City, Nevada: State Printing Office), chapter 4, p. 18.

27. Steele, Rufus, *Mustangs of the Mesa* (Hollywood, California: Press of Murray and Gee, 1941), p. 62.

28. Barnum, work cited in note 4 above, p. 288.

29. Ibid., p. 286.

30. Ibid., p. 288.

31. Ibid., pp. 286-287.

32. Grover, Jack, "Running Mustangs," *The Horse* (March-April, 1948), pp. 18-20.

33. Barnum, work cited in note 4 above, p. 302.

34. James, work cited in note 8 above, p. 209.

35. Steele, work cited in note 27 above, pp. 71-76.

36. Barnum, work cited in note 4 above, pp. 296-298.

37. Interview with Albert Laird, Dayton, Nevada.

38. Barnum, Charles P., "Trapping Wild Horses of the Nevada Desert at Night," *Eureka Sentinel* (June 11, 1910). See also Barnum, work cited in note 4 above, and Will James's chapter, "Pinyon and the Wild Ones," in work cited in note 8 above.

39. Steele, Rufus, "Trapping Wild Horses in Nevada," *McClure's Magazine* (December, 1909), pp. 128-209.

40. Ibid.

41. *Eureka Sentinel* (January 2, 1917).

42. "A Horseless Horseman," *Sunset Magazine* (May, 1914), pp. 1097-1101.

43. James, Will, *Cow Country* (New York: Grosset and Dunlap, n.d.), p. 16.

Chapter Four

1. Interview with Herman Smoot, Carson City, Nevada.

2. Rollins, Phillip Ashton, *The Cowboy* (New York: Scribner's, 1924), p. 281.

3. Hanks, Ed, *A Long Dust on the Desert* (Sparks, Nevada: privately printed, 1967), pp. 104-106.

4. Dobie, J. Frank, *A Vaquero of the Brush Country* (Boston: Little, Brown and Company, 1929), p. 226.

5. James, Will, *Cowboys North and South* (New York: Grosset and Dunlap, n.d.), p. 191.

6. Barnes, Will C., "Wild Horses," *McClure's Magazine* (January, 1909), p. 286.

7. Cook, James H., "Wild Horses of the Plains," *Natural History* (January, 1919), p. 107.

8. Interview with Archie Dewar, Elko, Nevada.

9. Letter to author from Harry E. Webb, Tujunga, California.

10. Bourliere, Francois, *The Natural History of Mammals* (New York: Knopf, 1964), p. 373

11. Webb, letter cited in note 9 above.

12. Interview with Herman Smoot, Carson City, Nevada.

13. Rojas, R. R., *California Vaquero* (Fresno, California: Academy Library Guild, 1953), p. 79.

14. Interview with Albert Laird, Dayton, Nevada.

15. Carrighar, Sally, *Wild Heritage* (New York: Houghton-Mifflin, 1965), p. 146.

16. Dobie, work cited in note 4 above, p. 228.

17. Tevis, William S., Jr., *The Horse* (San Francisco: privately printed, 1922), p. 62.

18. Hall, Edward T., "Territorial Needs and Limits," *Natural History* (December, 1965), pp. 12-19.

19. Bates, Marston, *The Forest and the Sea* (New York: Vintage, 1965), p. 202. See also Bourliere, chapter 3 of work cited in note 10 above.

20. James, Will, "The Prodigal's Return," *Sunset Magazine* (September, 1921), p. 41.

21. Letter to author from Lee Rice, San Leandro, California.

22. Interview with Ed Hanks, Fallon, Nevada.

23. Walker, Johnny, "The Wild Horses of Early California," *Western Horseman* (October, 1936), p. 26.

24. Interview with Frank Robbins, Glenrock, Wyoming.

25. Bearcraft, Norma, "Our Shameful Treatment of Wild Horses," *Bit and Bridle* (September-October, 1966), pp. 16, 26.

26. Lockhardt, Frank, "Black Kettle," in *Mustangs and Cow Hors-*

es, ed. by J. Frank Dobie, Moody C. Boatright, and Harry H. Hanson (Dallas: Southern Methodist University Press, second edition, 1965), p. 134.

27. James, work cited in note 5 above, p. 201.

28. Dobie, J. Frank, *The Mustangs* (Boston: Little, Brown and Company, 1952), p. 137.

29. Steele, Rufus, *Mustangs of the Mesa* (Hollywood, California: Press of Murray and Gee, 1941), p. 55.

30. Webb, work cited in note 9 above.

31. Steele, work cited in note 29 above, p. 57.

32. Interview with Walt James, Elko, Nevada.

Chapter Five

1. Oliver, Herman, *Gold and Cattle Country* (Portland: Binford and Morts, 1961), p. 146.

2. James, Will, *Cowboys North and South* (New York: Grosset and Dunlap, n.d.), p. 203.

3. "Grand Stallion Prefers Death to Servitude," *Tonopah Daily Bonanza* (August 16, 1913).

4. Steele, Rufus, *Mustangs of the Mesa* (Hollywood, California: Press of Murray and Gee, 1941), pp. 93-94.

5. Ibid., pp. 94-97.

6. Ibid., pp. 199-207, freely paraphrased.

7. Walgamott, Charles Shirley, *Six Decades Back* (Caldwell, Idaho: Caxton, 1936), pp. 267-272.

8. Letters to author from Harry E. Webb, Tujunga, California. Story printed in its entirety in *Frontier Times* (January, 1970), entitled "Old Spook."

9. "Journal of James Kenny," *Journal of American Folklore* (January-March, 1946), p. 55.

10. Military use of camels is described in *Uncle Sam's Camels,* by Lewis Burt Lesley (Cambridge: Harvard University Press, 1929). The Joggles Wright episode is in *Mark Twain in Nevada,* by Effie Mona Mack (New York: Scribner's, 1947), pp. 186-188.

11. "Camel Horses From Nevada," letter in *Western Horseman* (March, 1952), p. 8. Additional reporting in *The Pony Express* (Sonora, California, February, 1968), p. 11.

12. "Fur Covered Horses," letter in *Western Horseman* (May-June, 1947), p. 26.

13. Interview with Albert Laird, Dayton, Nevada. A few other in-

formants in Eureka, Nevada, recall hearing of Tom Dixon's fur covered horses and that they were imported by Dixon.

14. Interview with Tom Holland, President, National Mustang Association, Cedar City, Utah.

Chapter Six

1. Westermeier, Clifford P., compiler and editor, *Trailing The Cowboy* (Caldwell, Idaho: Caxton, 1955), pp. 93-94.

2. Twain, Mark, *Roughing It* (New York: Harper and Brothers, 1913), pp. 170-171.

3. Adams, Ramon, *Western Words* (Norman: University of Oklahoma Press, 1944). Freely synthesized.

4. Interview with Wallace I. "Bob" Robertson, Carson City, Nevada.

5. Reames, Wallace, "Catching and Holding the Green Colt," *Western Horseman* (August, 1949), pp. 22-23.

6. Adams, work cited in note 3 above, p. 20.

7. Interview with Joe De Young, Hollywood, California.

8. Hanks, Ed, *A Long Dust on the Desert* (Sparks, Nevada: privately printed, 1967), p. 24.

9. Ibid., p. 14.

10. Adams, work cited in note 3 above.

11. Hanks, work cited in note 8 above, p. 27.

12. Letter to the author from Al Erwin, Palm Springs, California.

13. *Elko Independent* (August 1, 1913).

14. Ibid. (August 15, 1913).

15. Ibid.

16. *Tonopah Daily Bonanza* (August 28, 1913).

17. Interview with Lillia Pepper, Dayton, Nevada.

18. McElrath, Jean, *Aged In Sage* (no city: privately printed, 1964), p. 71.

19. Interview with Jewell Martin, Carson City, Nevada.

20. "Wants Nevada Horses in Kentucky For Common People," *Ely Weekly Mining Expositor* (circa 1910).

Chapter Seven

1. "Last of Montana's Wild Horses Captured After Long Chase," *Tonopah Daily Bonanza* (July 31, 1919).

2. "A Nevada Industry," *Reno Gazette* (February 23, 1899).

3. "Hide Buyers," *Daily Independent* (Elko, October 18, 1897).

4. Barnes, Will C., "Wild Horses," *McClure's Magazine* (vol. XXXII, 1908-09), p. 285.

5. Ibid.

6. Roberts, Paul H., *Hoof Prints On The Range* (San Antonio: Naylor Co., 1963), p. 136.

7. Wyman, Walker D., *The Wild Horse of the West* (Caldwell, Idaho: Caxton, 1946), p. 204.

8. "Wild Horses For Chicken Feed," *Record Courier* (Gardnerville, December 10, 1926).

9. "Horses Shipped From Elko," *Record Courier* (Gardnerville, December 18, 1925).

10. Wyman, work cited in note 7 above, p. 205.

11. Kreuter, Adolph C., "I Herded The Wild Ones," *Frontier Times* (July, 1966), p. 30.

12. Ibid.

13. "Slaughter 40,000 Horses in Year For European Shipment," *Carson City Daily Appeal* (March 2, 1928).

14. Kreuter, work cited in note 11 above, p. 31.

15. Ibid., p. 30.

16. Lord Russell, "The Mustang Returns to Europe in Tin Cans," *Cattleman* (October, 1928).

17. Wyman, work cited in note 7 above, p. 207.

18. "2,000 Toiyabe Wild Horses Exterminated," *Eureka Sentinel* (April 7, 1928).

19. Interview with E. R. Greenslet, Reno, Nevada.

20. History of the Taylor Grazing Act is told in *Politics and Grass,* by Phillip O. Foss (Seattle: University of Washington Press, 1970). Problems peculiar to Nevada are stated in *The Taylor Grazing Act in Nevada,* Bulletin 76 (Reno: Agricultural Extension Service, University of Nevada, 1935). See also "Horses and the Taylor Grazing Act" in *Western Horseman* (May-June, 1940), and "Modoc County Cattle History," *California Cattleman* (December, 1966).

21. Roberts, work cited in note 6 above, pp. 137-138.

22. Wyman, work cited in note 7 above, pp. 171-172.

23. Anonymous; presently in state government service.

24. Interview with Albert Laird, Dayton, Nevada.

25. Interview with Darrell Fullwidder, Berkeley, California (formerly with Bureau of Land Management in Reno, Nevada).

26. Greenslet, interview cited in note 19 above.

27. "Flying Machine to Corral Wild Horses," *Weekly Independent* (Elko, May 12, 1912).

28. Letter to Editor, "Aerial Cowboy," *Life* (July 25, 1938).